STEAMING AMBITIONS

THE FOOTPLATE RECOLLECTIONS OF A PRESTON ENGINEMAN

BY
BOB JACKSON

TRIANGLE

PUBLISHING

Copyright @ Triangle Publishing and R.Jackson 1999.

British Library Cataloguing in Publication Data.

Jackson R.

Steaming Ambitions.

ISBN 0-952-9333-49

Printed in Great Britain by the Amadeus Press Ltd, Huddersfield.

Text by Bob Jackson.

Edited & assisted by Mick Howarth.

Edited for publication by D.J.Sweeney.

Compiled by Triangle Publishing.

Cover design by Scene, Print & Design, Leigh, Ltd.

Designed and Published by

Triangle Publishing,

509, Wigan Road,

Leigh, Lancs. Tel/Fax.01942/677919

Front Cover. 'Britannia' No.70018 *Flying Dutchman* awaits its next turn of duty at Preston c1963. Photo, P.J.Fitton,Colour Rail.

Rear Cover.

B.R Standard No.70022 *Tornado* heads south through Wigan North Western with a freight in March 1967.   B.Magilton.

Lostock Hall on 2nd August 1968. In a few days steam would be withdrawn and scenes like this but a memory.   D.Hill.

Plate 1 A view at Spring Branch on 16th October 1962, with 'Royal Scot' No.46159 *The Royal Air Force.*
Photo, W.D.Cooper.

CONTENTS

Plate 2. A view inside the roofless Preston Shed on 26th October 1961 with 'Coronation' Pacific No.46257, *City of Salford* at rest.

Photo, J.A.Oldfield.

FORWARD

Railway history is a vast subject which encompasses varied subjects ranging from the mechanical intricacies of locomotives with their endless variety of design, evolution and rebuilds to the planning and building of the lines themselves by private railway companies of the last century. Books on these subjects must be technically and historically correct as the facts are unchangeable. Books and articles on the equally important subject of railway operation, especially the day to day workings do not need to have the same amount of research put into them as technical correctness does not enter into the subject to the same degree. This does not mean, however, that the facts are not true just that they can be written in a more entertaining way.

The railways of Britain have now come full circle from their early beginnings as private companies through what many would regard as their golden age, then to the steady decline of grouping and nationalisation back to the hope of restoring some semblence of prosperity with the reprivatisation of recent times.

This book tells of one mans experiences working on the steam locomotives of British Railways. This is not one of the technical or factual histories but it is railway history none the less. That there is a demand for this type of book was illustrated to me when, as the then publisher of "Northern Railways" magazine, I persuaded Mr. Jackson to write a number of articles relating his footplate experiences.This proved to be one of the most popular series of articles published in the magazine and it was from this favourable response that the first ideas of a possible book took root.

The author relates how his early interest in railways grew to the point where the only career he was interested in was one with British Railways. He finishes with the last days of steam in 1968, and although Mr. Jackson did carry on with his footplate career in the diesel and electric era of the 70's, 80's and 90's, we get a look at what life was really like on the footplate of working steam in it's final years.

Mick Howarth.

INTRODUCTION

It is now some two years since I retired from railway service, after spending almost forty years of footplate workings on a variety of steam, diesel and electric locomotives.

During these years I have always kept a diary of daily events, not just of unusual happenings but also the more mundane and everyday events that occured. One day a visiting friend who was also a railway enthusiast read one of these diaries and suggested to me the idea of writing a book based on my footplate experiences. This thought had never crossed my mind until then but the idea began to take root. As with so many other people in the same position, retirement had left me with a lot of spare time to kill. To fill some of these idle hours I began doodling with the first skeleton outline of this volume.

At first I thought no one would be interested in reading such a book but after completing a couple of chapters reaction from those who read it seemed encouraging so I pressed on. As commented by one enthusiast, it is important to get these everyday experiences down on paper before they are forgotten altogether with the passage of time. Indeed there are many entries in my diaries which give information such as locomotive, working and driver but I cannot remember any details about the days events as they occured so long ago as they have vanished from my memory. The events related in this book are just some that have for some reason stuck in my mind.

I hope that readers of this book will find it entertaining. I certainly enjoyed writing it. This is what daily life on the footplate was really like. Unglamorous, dirty and hard work, but the people who had to carry out these tasks where some of the finest men you could meet and each one had a character of his own to make the work more bearable and fun. I wouldn't have missed it for the world and all I can say to the men of the footplate on todays modern railway is keep up the good work.

Bob Jackson,
Chorley, Lancs. 1999

Plate 3. The Author seen in the cab of A.C.Electric, Class 86, No.86 213 *Lancashire Witch* at Preston c1984, about to depart with a northbound express.

Photo, Mick Howarth.

CHAPTER ONE
THE EARLY YEARS

My love of railway locomotives began in the early fifties at the age of seven when all my mates began train spotting. I will never forget that first sunny day at Euxton Coal Sidings on the West Coast Main Line where we all met armed to the teeth with pens, notepads, pop, sandwiches and the Ian Allan, Locospotters "Bible". At first there was four of us, Paul Tuson, Raymond Scard and Mick Howarth (who all later became footplatemen at Lostock Hall shed) and myself but it soon increased to over fifteen dedicated bodies.

My first locomotive for the book was a rather grimy looking Black Five, (known to us as a Mickey) No. 45454 from Preston shed working a southbound mixed freight. The rest of the day saw a mixture of different locomotive classes including Patriots, Jubilees, Royal Scots, Austerities and Black Eights..

The Up and Down "Royal Scots" were headed by Coronation Pacific No. 46226 *Duchess of Norfolk* and the twin diesels Nos 10000-10001. It was from that first memorable day that I realised what glorious and majestic machines the steam locomotives were and what kings the drivers and firemen were in charge of their steeds, with names like *Agamemnon, Planet, The Loyal Regiment* and *Princess Alexandra.*

All to soon the day was over and it was time to go back home. It was a very excited and contented lad that went to bed that night. After two or three more visits to local spots it became apparent that to see more variety we would have to travel farther afield, to places like York, in order to see the East Coast locomotives with names after racehorses like *Salmon Trout, Ladas, Harvester* and *Victor Wild.* Next it was over to the Western Region to see the Kings, Castles, Halls, Manors and Counties with their splendid brass safety valves and copper capped chimneys that gleamed in the sunshine, (its a pity they did not know how to build a cab roof). On the Southern Region we took note of the powerful Merchant Navy Class with names like *Port Line, Elders Fyffes* and *Belgian Marine.* Soon my 10/6d Ian Allan combined volume was filling up fast with lines under the numbers and names (I never did manage to fill the book) as we ventured far and wide across the country to the stations and engine sheds both large and small in our quest to catch the rare ones. By this time I had made up my mind that footplate work was the career I wanted to pursue on leaving St George's school in Chorley, but this was not to be, although my father did his best, (probably after getting ear-ache with my pestering) to get me on at Springs Branch Shed, Wigan. The only thing we heard from the shed master was "Sorry we have no vacancies at this time but should one arise we'll let you know." Being in need of work at that time I took a job as an apprentice stripper and grinder at the Cowling Ring Mill in Chorley but my heart was still set on the footplate.

That mill was like a prison as every day went by, the only consolation being that it was situated near the Manchester-Preston line and at 10.45 each morning the 10.10am. Manchester to Glasgow express would come hurtling through on it's way. Haulage was usually a 'Clan' but you could expect anything from a Jubilee, Royal Scot or Britannia class at the front end. Most of the people in the mill knew of my obsession with the railway and tried to make my life as easy as possible. One day I was allowed to go into the mill engine room to see the mighty steam engine that ran the mill machinery via shafts running the full length of the large rooms for six or seven storeys.

That day was another highlight for me as I never knew a steam engine could be so big, it's two massive cylinders driving an even more massive flywheel. Each of the cylinders had a name; one was *Samson* and the other *Goliath*. They looked splendid as they were kept polished and gleaming. Once I was in this room they had a job to get me out, so I asked the manager if I could work with the engine but he told me the mill was unfortunately going to close down soon and he wanted me to complete my apprenticeship in order to be qualified when I moved, so back to the rattling carding machines I went after the best day of my life in the mill.

Two months later I completed my apprenticeship and became qualified at my unchosen job and the manager was indeed right because the Cowling Mill closed one week later. I along with many others was transferred to the ring spinning mill at Coppull which was more convenient for me as I lived in the village and could walk to work in ten minutes or so. Coppull Ring Mill is situated alongside the West Coast Main Line and still stands today but is now Coppull Enterprise Centre with units of shops and a public house called the Lakeside Inn taking over what used to be the administration building, but in the late fifties it was a bustling place of work.

Most of my spare time and dinner hours were taken up at the mill window watching the locomotives rushing past with their different types of trains with coal, cattle, milk, pigeons, parcels and passengers, and other merchandise that was needed to keep the country running smoothly day in and day out. Oh how I envied those locomen dashing about the country working the steam engines in their blue overalls and greasetop caps.

At this time I became friendly with another lad named Peter Worthington who lived in nearby Standish and he too was fed-up with working in the mill and wanted different employment outside the cotton industry and the first chance he got he was out for good as his job was worse than mine, working the lift up and down from one floor to another.

One day during my dinner hour I was talking to a Wigan girl, Margaret Prescott, and during conversation she informed me that her boyfriend was a fireman at Springs Branch Shed. This was the chance I had been waiting for, a contact with someone in the railway industry. I asked her if she would have a word with him about my plight and keep his eyes open for any vacancies that may crop up in the future for engine cleaners and it was left at that. To my surprise and delight five weeks later Margaret came over to me all excited and told me that her boyfriend had noticed there were vacancies for cleaners at Preston Shed starting the following week. Margaret's boyfriend said to tell me that I was to go and get my name down the following day or so. My next task was to inform my friend Peter of the news as he was keen to go with me to try himself for a job on the footplate.

On finishing our shift that day, Peter and I went to see our boss, Mr Frank Yates, about having the following day off for some urgent business. He replied with a knowing smile; "Don't tell me you've got a job on the locomotives at last, I've known about it for weeks. Have the day off and good luck to both of you." For this we thanked him and went home to tell our parents.

My father had passed away two months earlier so it was my hard pressed mother who received this (to me) monumental news. Obviously not as impressed by the developments of the past couple of days as I was, she simply asked what I would do if I didn't get the job on the railway. This was a possibility that had not even crossed my mind, the thought of which was unbearable and my answer was rapid; " Then I'll stay in the mill until I rot."

The following morning Peter called for me and away to Preston we went by train from the now closed Coppull Station. On arrival at the motive power depot we reported to the Shedmaster, Mr Grant, who informed us both that vacancies for cleaners did indeed exist at the depot but the pay for cleaners was not very much although promotion was fairly rapid and the pay went up accordingly as you climbed the tree. He also informed us that we would have to undergo a strict medical examination for hearing, general health and most important of all, eyesight, as you are not much use on the footplate if you are colour blind and tone deaf. We both agreed and on that note he told us to report for duty one week the following Monday.

On Friday, we both gave one weeks notice to the mill manager to which he commented, "I'm very happy for you both and I'll give each of you a reference for your new employer on your prompt timekeeping whilst employed at the mill." And with those words he accepted our resignations.

That last week at Coppull Ring Mill seemed like months but our workmates kept us busy to try and make the time pass quickly. They really were a fantastic bunch of people and I will never forget them for their kindness and understanding shown to two lads who wanted to work on the railway. Also at this time I must say a big thank you to Margaret and her boyfriend without whose help I would not have got the job I so badly wanted from leaving school.

On Thursday of that last week at the mill, Mr Yates came to see us both and told us to report to the engine room for the day as two of the men were having a day off and we could help by keeping the thing clean, and at the same time it might prepare us for our job the following week. Working in the engine room was not a job, it was more like sheer bliss and I don't think we could have put more enthusiasm in the spit and polish if we had tried. We rubbed and scrubbed until our arms ached but we were happy and it was sad when the hooter blew at five-o'-clock to end the shift. On arrival home my mother took one look at me and said; "Where have you been, you look like an oil rag,' to which I replied; " They have had me working in the engine room for the day to keep it clean." " Well it should be clean now because most of it is on you." (Little did she know what was to come.)

At last it was Friday and our very last day at the mill, and what a day that was with all the farewells and the "Don't forget to give us a blow on the whistle when you pass." I was also presented with one of the most beautiful railway books I have ever seen and everyone signed it inside the front cover making it a most cherished possession to this day.

Plate 4. One of Sir William Stanier's 'Jubilee' class locomotives No.45698, *Mars*, rolls into Preston station about 1960 with an excursion special for the Fylde Coast. These locomotives were introduced by the L.M.S. in 1934 and originally classified as 5XP. Under the British Railways regime they were classed as 6P5F. A number of enginemen referred to the 'Jubilees' as indifferent steamers, some good, some bad. As such they were not regarded as one of the best ex- L.M.S. designs.

Photo, Alex Mann.

CHAPTER TWO
THE CLEANERS LOT

At 9am on a wet and miserable morning we reported for duty at Preston Shed for our very first day on the railway. The date was 17th October 1960, and our first task was to look around the shed and find out where everything was located such as the fitters room, stores, sand bin, coaling plant, ash pit, disposers cabin and what seemed like a thousand and one other places.

Our guide on this tour was another cleaner who showed us all the nooks and crannies. His name was Mick Sunter; he had started two weeks previously so he knew where he was going as Peter and I did not know one end of the shed from the other. Our next task was to each have a locker assigned to us and we were given some old overalls until we were issued with a set of new ones. Next it was back to the office to receive our all important pay check numbers. I was allocated the number 337 and it was a number I must not forget because everything arriving at the shed with that number was mine (Including pay).

Now we had to meet the Foreman Cleaner, an oldish gentleman named Bill Ashe, an ex driver who was now in charge of all the cleaners at Preston Shed. He told them which locomotive had to be cleaned , and when, and generally tried to keep order amongst an unruly mob of cleaners, namely Jim Hoggarth, Alan Pitcher, Paul Ryan, Kevin Mitchel, Tony Holman and Brian Townsend to name just a few. For some reason the cleaning gangs at every steam shed seemed to be a collection of the most mischevious and uncontrollable individuals, whose main aim in life was to cause disruption and chaos wherever they went.

All to soon it was time to finish our first day as employees of British Railways. When we signed off duty we were told to report at the same time the following day in order to attend a medical examination at Preston Station scheduled for 9.45am with Dr. Read. After signing on duty we made our way to the medical centre located on platform 9, arriving at 9.35am. to be greeted by Dr. Read who was a well spoken gentleman and also a keen railway enthusiast and photographer. Mine was the first name called out and I was ushered into a black painted room with just a small light in the middle. Once inside this strange room a pair of headphones was put over my ears and I was told to raise my hand when I heard any bleeps. This part of the test must have proved satisfactory because in no time at all the headphones were removed. Next it was the eye test and the first requirement was to read a graph with the letters gradually becoming smaller (As you see in any opticians room today) with one eye blanked off and then the process repeated with the other eye. Next the light was turned off and a small lantern lit at the far end of the room showing different coloured lights of white ,yellow, red and green and I had to say which colour was showing at every change. That over, I was shown a book that at first glance looked like nothing but a mass of coloured dots but on closer examination revealed a number hidden in the dots on every page except one. Now the eyesight test was over and I was shown to a cubicle and told to strip then make my way to the doctors surgery where he checked my lungs, heart etc. Some twenty minutes later I was back in the waiting room being told that I had satisfactorily passed my medical and to report back to the shed. I waited at the medical centre until Peter had completed his examination so we could both return together.

It was a sad Peter Worthington that emerged from the medical centre as he explained that they had found a fault with his left eye and he had failed the medical for footplate duties. He did however, start work as timekeeper in Wigan No. I signal box and later became a signalman on the Whelley route which by-passed Wigan to the East.

Preston Shed was situated just north of the station, on the left hand side of Fylde Junction. This site now houses the Preston power signalbox and Croft Street Sidings but in those days it was an eleven road steam locomotive shed that housed a variety of freight and passenger locomotives

The locomotives included two 0-4-0 saddletank shunting engines Nos.47002 and 47008 for working the Greenbank Yard with its very tight curves; 0-6-0 Jinties for working Ribble, North Union and Dock Street yards as well as the station pilots. Some ex L.N.W.R. 0-8-0 Super D's (Known to us as night fighters) for the l in 29 Preston Dock branch. A Hughes 'Crab', 'Black 5' 4-6-0's, for both passenger and freight duties with Standard and ex L.M.S. 2-6-0's used for station pilot duties when this required steam heating equipment to be used. Two 'Jubilee' 4-6-0's Nos.45582 *Central Provinces* and 45633 *Aden*, for Windermere, Barrow and Manchester work along with three 7P,4-6-0 'Royal Scots' Nos. 46161 *King s Own*, 46165 *The Ranger (12th London Regt)* and 46168, *The Girl Guide* used on the London workings. In summer the shed could be host to 60 or 70 locomotives including those from other depots such as Crewe and Carlisle.

Most of our days as cleaners were spent either working on the coaling plant, ash-pit, or as fitters labourers doing such jobs as shovelling spilled coal back into a wagon. It was extremely hard work but after a few days it seemed to get easier as your body got used to the toil and your muscles built up. One of the cleaners, Tony Holman, nearly always took on the job as barlad, who had the task of changing the firebars on dead locomotives. This was a very dirty and thankless job that entailed crawling into the firebox through the firehole door in order to change the badly twisted or worn firebars. On occasions the other cleaners spotted him working on a locomotive and decided to 'smoke him out.' This 'joke' was achieved by sneaking onto the footplate armed with some oily rags, setting them on fire and throwing them into the firebox then closing the firehole doors. The noise emanating from the unfortunate individual inside that box was alarming as Tony tried frantically to beat out the flames and fight his way out via the ashpan into the pit beneath looking like a denizen from below with a black face and streaming, bright red eyes.

Sometimes a tender locomotive would need it's tender water tank cleaning out to remove coal and debris that had accidentally dropped in via the filler hole and could block the injector pipe.

Once the water was drained out a cleaner was sent in via a ladder to clean it out with a firing

Plate 5. 'Royal Scot' No.46161, *Kings Own* seen beneath the roofless Preston Shed on 28th November 1960, as the cleaning gang pose for the camera.On the extreme left, yours truly, but the chap beside me is unknown. Seated is Alan Pitcher, then Mick Sunter, Paul Ryan and Jim Hoggart

Photo, Authors collection.

Plate 6. Nearly two years later 46161, *Kings Own* is again seen at Preston Shed being prepared to work the southbound 'Lakes Express' from Preston to Euston on a miserable day in 1963. The shed roof had been destroyed by fire on 28th June 1960.

Photo, Dave Dyson.

shovel and bucket. Once inside the tank the other cleaners pounced like wild cats onto the back of the tender with their oily rags and when lit, these too went into the tank, the ladder was removed, tank filler lid slammed shut and secured with a large piece of coal placed on top. As the tank was empty the echoing noise inside was far worse than in the firebox as the poor victim had no other way out.

One day I was introduced to a driver named Jim Cox who was the branch secretary of the trade union and he enrolled me as a member of the locomens union A.S.L.E & F. During our dinner break in the messroom I observed a notice on the wall, fastened with a drawing pin which I removed and placed it on the bench seat next to me as I began to read the article. I had just started reading when a driver came over and sat down. He almost hit the roof as the pin stuck solidly into his rear end swearing to hang whoever had put it on the seat, needless to say I didn't own up to this and beat a hasty retreat to safety.

Just inside the shed entrance was a very large sand bin about 10ft high and 6 or 7ft in diameter with a low fire underneath in order to keep the sand dry for the locomotives. One morning a cleaner who had obviously had a rough night out the previous evening decided it would make a very nice and cozy bed out of sight of everyone in which to have a couple of hours kip. Borrowing a ladder he climbed into the bin that was half full of sand and started what he thought was going to be an enjoyable experience on warm sand. He should have known better, the cleaners always managed to find out if some poor individual had put himself in a vulnerable position, making a suitable prey to their antics. The roaming gang of miscreants soon gathered round the sand bin to formulate their plan. The ladder was first removed, the fire stoked up and about 15 or 20 buckets of sand removed from the bottom. This action lowered the lad further inside the bin as the sand was taken away until there was no hope of him climbing out. Some ten minutes later all hell broke loose as he started to roast in the confined space, half full of baking sand getting hotter and hotter by the minute. What a job it was to retrieve him and we all received a full ticking off from the shedmaster but how he ever explained what he was doing there in the first place I will never know. These antics by the cleaners went on day in and day out as they constantly looked for ways to play tricks on any unfortunate individual who they decided to turn their attention upon.

On Thursdays,all the men at the shed were issued with a one and a half inch diameter brass disc with their personal number stamped on it. This had to be handed to the pay clerk after lunch time in order to receive their wages in a tin. One day I received my disc in the morning but managed to lose it within two hours and no matter where I looked it was nowhere to be found. I had to report to the shift foreman who was not at all amused and he said that I would have to take the 'lost check'. I had never seen one before but I was soon to find out that it was another disc but about 1 in thick and 3in diameter made of lead with a piece of string attached.

The whole lump was placed around my neck and I was not to remove it until pay out time and from that day on I never lost my pay check again.

Plate 7 An undated view across the main lines from below Preston No.5 signalbox shows 'Coronation' Pacific 4-6-2, No.46226, *Duchess of Norfolk* taking water prior to working a southbound express.　　Photo, Paul Tuson.

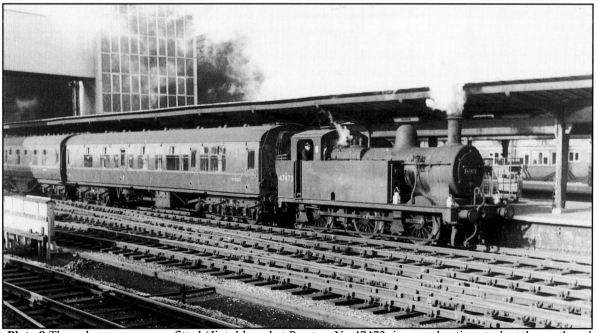

Plate 8 The only screw reverse fitted 'Jinty' based at Preston, No.47472, is seen shunting stock at the south end of Preston Station whilst on station pilot duties on 20th April 1966. This locomotive was transferred to Lostock Hall Shed following closure of Preston Shed in 1961.　　Photo, Mick Howarth.

Another time on a rather cold winters morning we recieved our first steam lance trom Crewe works, a device used for cleaning the motion on locomotives. It was a very long rubber pipe, wound with wire on it's full length and fitted with a tapered nozzle on one end and a brass nut on the other to fasten to a steam valve located on the front ofthe locomotive smokebox. We could not wait to try this useful cleaning aid on a Black Five, so as soon as it was out of the stores wagon we carried it off to the locomotive which was to be the subject of our attention. I coupled it up while Jim Hoggarth held on to the business end. I heard him shout "OK TURN IT ON;" so turn it on I did by opening the valve as far as it would open !

At first nothing appeared to happen, then I heard all the other cleaners screaming and shouting to "TURN IT OFF". On looking down the side of the locomotive all I could see was a huge balloon shape looming at the back of Jim which one second later exploded with an almighty bang that would have stirred the dead. Jim let his end drop and ran like the clappers as the pipe whipped about all over the shed floor. I was so transfixed by this sight that I forgot to turn it off bolting for cover with the rest of the 'gang'. The foreman cleaner swore that we would never again receive another steam lance, just a bucket of blue dick (A mixture of oil and parafffin) and a dozen half dirty rags.

A couple of weeks later Bill Ashe retired as foreman cleaner and was replaced by a short, thick set man named Billy Moat who did not want us cleaning unless it was absoluteley necessary but would rather we worked on the coaling plant and ash pit, or with the fitters etc.

One Monday morning he armed us all with picks and told us to break up the old air raid shelter that was situated just outside the shed entrance as best we could. No matter how hard we hit it, it was like trying to knock down a wall with a toffee hammer. One of the cleaners, Paul Ryan, said he had a brilliant idea, providing we could get hold of some newspapers and oily rags. Thus we all set off to require the necessary items and soon returned with great bundles from the shed and local paper shops. This was soon joined with wood, coal and any other combustible material that was not bolted down. Some five minutes later Paul returned with about ten boxes of detonators, "What the hell do we need those for?" we all asked, "Never mind" he replied, just put them all inside the shelter and fill it up with the rest of the stuff. This we did and waited to see what was next. Soon some paraffn was sneaked out of the oil stores and he commenced to pour it all over the mixture in the shelter. "Now lads, if this doesn't make it collapse nothing will"! All we need to do now is burn it to the ground. Before we could speak he had lit the paper at the entrance and we all stood well clear, at first nothing appeared to happen but two minutes later all hell broke loose as the detonators exploded, out shot all the debris, breaking five shed windows in the process. All the cleaners vanished like sewer rats a matter of seconds before the foreman, shedmaster, fitters, drivers and Billy Moat arrived on the scene with Billy screaming that he would kill the lot of us, but nobody was in sight. Before signing off duty that day we were all frog-marched into Mr Gants office to receive the sternest telling off and being told that the next time repair money would be taken out of our wages.

Another amusing incident occured one Friday morning as we all sat down to a cup of tea in the messroom. Billy Moat who had been sitting with us decided to visit the toilet and while he was away one of the lads embarked on a plan to test his reaction. One of the cleaners was placed at the door to await his return and give a signal to the others when he came into sight. Some ten minutes later the signal was given so Mick Sunter dropped two Alka Seltzers into his pint cup of steaming hot tea. All Billy saw on his return was his cuppa frothing all over the table top like something out of a science fiction movie, he must have been watching that cup for fifteen minutes before he tossed the lot down the sink thinking it was a witches brew, (He never did find out what caused it).

Plate 9. Former Western Region 'Britannia' No.70025, *Western Star* is seen coasting down the bank from Charnock Richard to Balshaw Lane with a northbound express in the 1960's. Before being transferred to the London Midland Region of B.R., the locomotive had been based at Cardiff Canton, working Western Region expresses to Paddington. It can ascertained that this is one of the Ex Western Britannias by the number of handholes cut into the smoke deflectors, six in total. This modification came about after an accident involving No 70026 *Polar Star* at Milton near Didcot on 22nd November 1955. It was suggested at the subsequent inquiry that the handrails, as fitted originally, had impaired the drivers forward vision, hence this variation. The Eastern Region only fitted two handholes plus a small additional horizontal handrail. Those Britannias allocated to the L.M.R. never received any modification. Photo, Paul Tuson.

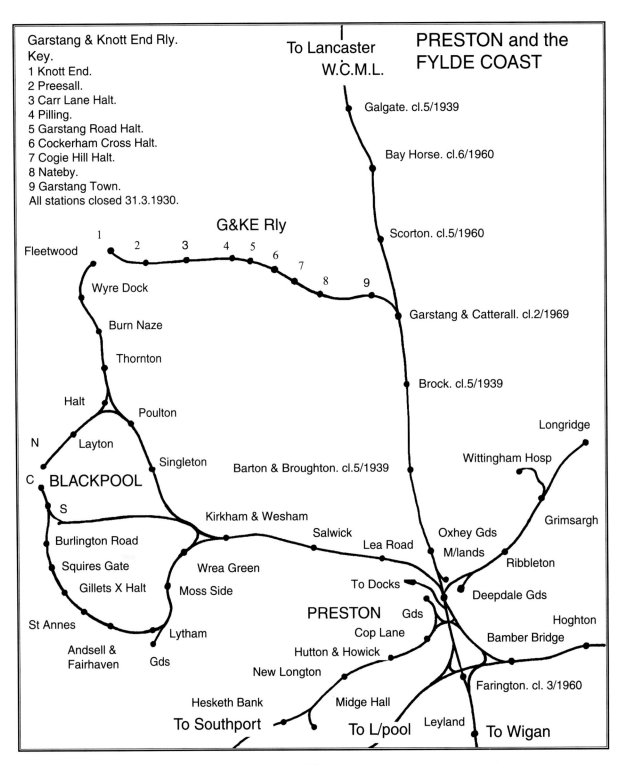

Garstang & Knott End Rly.
Key.
1 Knott End.
2 Preesall.
3 Carr Lane Halt.
4 Pilling.
5 Garstang Road Halt.
6 Cockerham Cross Halt.
7 Cogie Hill Halt.
8 Nateby.
9 Garstang Town.
All stations closed 31.3.1930.

PRESTON and the
FYLDE COAST

To Lancaster
W.C.M.L.

Galgate. cl.5/1939

Bay Horse. cl.6/1960

Scorton. cl.5/1960

G&KE Rly

Fleetwood

Wyre Dock

Burn Naze

Thornton

Halt

Poulton

N

Layton

C

BLACKPOOL

S

Singleton

Burlington Road

Squires Gate

Gillets X Halt

St Annes

Andsell &
Fairhaven

Gds

Lytham

Moss Side

Wrea Green

Kirkham & Wesham

Barton & Broughton. cl.5/1939

Garstang & Catterall. cl.2/1969

Brock. cl.5/1939

Longridge

Wittingham Hosp

Grimsargh

Salwick

Lea Road

Oxhey Gds

M/lands

Ribbleton

To Docks

Deepdale Gds

PRESTON

Gds

Hoghton

Cop Lane

Bamber Bridge

Hutton & Howick

New Longton

Faringation. cl. 3/1960

Hesketh Bank

Midge Hall

To Southport

To L/pool

Leyland

To Wigan

18

CHAPTER THREE
FIRING SCHOOL

One Monday on a cold November morning we were told to report to the firing instructor who had arrived from Liverpool to teach us the basic ways of firing a locomotive. He was a grand old gentleman by the name of George Hearse but he looked rather stern in his long black raincoat and black trilby. We soon had no worries because he turned out to be one of the nicest people we have ever met and just wanted to get on with the task in hand. His first move was to take us into a makeshift classroom on Preston Station and explain about the firebox, boiler, smokebox, lip-plate, brick arch, tube plate, lead plugs and dampers. Next came the boiler tubes, regulator valve, safety valves and injectors before moving on to the smokebox with the blower, petticoat pipe, blast pipe and superheater element. We were all given a small book entitled "Controlled Firing" and George explained about combustion and the build up of clinker on the fire grate. Next he explained to us about the boiler and how it was not clever to have the locomotive blowing off as it was a waste of coal, water and our own energy. Also, he emphasised the point of not making black smoke.

Following our stint in the classroom he took us back to the shed for our first taste of handling the firing shovel. This was carried out on a 'dead' Black Five that had just had it's boiler washed on number nine road and was now awaiting the steam raiser. We all in turn took hold of the shovel and tried to shoot a shovel full of coal to the far end of the firebox. Our first attempts were a total disaster as about three pieces went into the box and the rest went all over the footplate floor. Some of us actually missed the hole altogether and hit the lip-plate instead sending a sudden jolt up our arms as the shovel came to a dead stop on hitting solid metal. After several attempts we all began to get the hang of it (With George's help of course) and reckoned we could manage any working the railway threw at us. Little did we know how wrong we were. Next we went onto a 'Live' Jubilee in order to set and work the injectors to replenish the water in the boiler. Once again it became a total disaster as every time we tried all we got was a blast of steam out of the overflow pipe and no water in the boiler. Eventually after careful manipulation of the injector regulator valve we soon obtained the required results and the injector began to sing as water began to rush through the cones on it's way to the top of the boiler and in via the clack. On finishing our first day with George he informed us that for the rest of the week we would be going out on the road for some practical experience on a moving locomotive hauling a passenger train to see how we stood up to it.

Tuesday morning saw six apprehensive cleaners booking on duty at 7am and meeting up with George in the drivers lobby in readiness for some proper work at last. He explained that we would be riding with the 8.15am. to Windermere, but first we had to prepare the locomotive which was standing on number four road. The locomotive in question was one of our own Jubilee 4-6-0s No.45633 *Aden*, and arriving at the engine we met our driver for the day Gilbert

Harris, who was a pleasant chap in his late fifties. The first job was to check the water in the boiler with the test cock on the water gauge, as you opened it the water would rush out of the glass and when closed again would return to it's normal level. The water was just bobbing below the top nut, so that was o.k. and as the boiler pressure gauge was showing 170psi we needed to spread the fire that had been piled up under the door by the steam raiser. This operation was carried out with the paddle, an all metal shovel with a ten foot long handle that was carried in the fire irons compartment on the tender. Just manoeuvring this implement out of the long hole and around the limited space inside the cab was a performance in it's own right but once accomplished it could be placed in the firebox and the fire spread all over the grate area. Some ten minutes later with a nice bed of coal burning through on all the grate, the safety valves began to feather as boiler pressure crept up to the maximum of 225lb psi and now we could test the injectors. As soon as we had finished all these tasks to prepare the engine and we were ready to leave the shed it was time to take off the handbrake for Gilbert and place the lamps on the bottom middle brackets to denote "Light Engine". While this was taking place Gilbert started to screw the locomotive into reverse gear ready to proceed tender first to the station. Once back on board, the vacuum brake was released and after a pop on the whistle the regulator was eased open. With a roar of escaping steam from the open cylinder drain cocks the massive 6' 9" driving wheels began to turn as we headed towards the ringing out cabin.

Upon arrival at the cabin I was the one elected to go on the telephone to the signalman in Preston No.5 box because I was standing nearest to the door. After ringing the signalbox code in a sort of morse like * *-* * I told the signalman that the locomotive for the 8.15 Windermere was ready to come off shed, to which he replied, "OK, your stock is in platform three". A matter of seconds later the points went over and the ground signal came off with a loud 'CLUNK.' Another pop on the whistle and we set off onto the Main Line to drop down the grade into the station.

Waiting in platform three stood seven coaches and once the locomotive was buffered up we all got a chance to "Hook On" as another part of our training. Hooking the heavy shackle on to the first coach hook did not seem too hard but getting the bottom lugs together on the vacuum and steam heating pipes was a different kettle of fish. Both ends of these pipes were fitted with bent opposing lugs and if you did not place them fully home the top bars would only fit half way and splitting them again took the strength of Mr Universe. A tap with the coal hammer sometimes managed to seperate them but you also stood the risk of breaking the lugs off altogether and having to wait for a new pipe to be fitted by the maintenance staff, and a possible late departure of the train. Following the hooking on procedure the lamp had to be taken off the tender and arranged on the front as one white light over each buffer to denote express passenger train.

Now it was back on the footplate to open the steam heat cock and put 40psi of steam into the train to keep the passengers warm. George decided that out of the six of us two would fire the locomotive to Lancaster, two from there to Oxenholme and two to the end of the journey at Windermere,with the same arrangement on the return journey back to Preston. Jim Hoggarth and myself were elected to do the first part of the run so the other four deposited themselves in the train and left us to it. Following the toss of a coin and Jim winning, I was told to fire the locomotive first as far as Garstang & Catterall and he would take it the rest of the way to Lancaster. My next job was to build up the fire under the door and back corners in readiness for the off as the station clock now showed 8.13am.

Two minutes later the right away was given and the signal was showing a clear road as far as the enormous signal gantry situated just North of Preston station. With *Aden* in full forward gear and the vacuum brake off, Gilbert gave a mighty upward heave on the regulator handle and slammed the lever controlling the cylinder drains shut with his foot as we started out of the station on the first leg of our journey. At the gantry, both home and distant signals were off for the West Coast Main Line and once past the shed and under Pedder Street bridge the reverser was screwed back to 50% and the regulator opened fully as the locomotive took to it like something alive. The three cylinder beat crashed out as we stormed past Oxheys Cattle Dock as I started the test of firing a locomotive on the move.

Firing a locomotive standing on shed is one thing but out on the Main Line it is another experience altogether. As I opened the firehole doors the fire was no longer red but pure white and the heat was almost unbearable. On shed everything was still for you to judge your swing with the shovel but now the back of the locomotive was whipping from left to right as the front of the tender went from right to left, so trying to get the coal from the tender, through a small hole and where you wanted it on a large 31 square foot grate area seemed an almost impossible task to me as my first three shovelfulls missed altogether and showered all over the floor and coal dust flew in all directions. Practice makes perfect they always say and in my case it was no exception and I discovered that standing with both feet on the locomotive and not with one on the tender front my body was only moving one way at a time so making it easier to hit the firehole.

Soon I was managing to reach the far end of the box, but placing it in the back corners tended to burn the back of my right hand. Gilbert's own fireman who was also on the footplate came over and explained that the trick was to put some coal directly under the door first to slightly deaden the fire where your right hand ended up with the shovel. In no time at all I had a good bed of fire in the box and with the firehole doors almost closed the safety valves began to lift slightly and as the boiler water had now dropped to half full in the gauge glass, I operated the exhaust steam injector and sat down on the fireman's seat awash in sweat, but to feel the cold air hitting my face seemed like heaven.

I had been sat down for no more than thirty seconds when Gilbert yelled "WATER TROUGHS," so I was up again to the other side of the cab facing the water pick-up apparatus located on the tender front as the other three bodies in the cab stood well clear."NOW" shouted the driver and I frantically turned the wheel clockwise to lower the scoop into the trough. A matter of seconds later he shouted again "TAKE IT OUT" but no matter how I pulled on that wheel it would not budge. On seeing my dilemma, Gilbert immediately stood on his seat. George stood on the fireman's seat and his fireman climbed on the tender shelf leaving just Jim and myself stood in total confusion on the footplate floor. We soon found out why as about fifty gallons of water suddenly rushed into the cab from all directions almost drowning us both, not to mention the couple of hundred gallons that cascaded over the first three coaches. That was undoubtedly another lesson I learned the hard way. Don't wait for the driver to shout but keep your eye on the tank filler gauge and when almost full to take the scoop out. All too soon I was just getting into the hang of it when Gilbert put on the blower, opened the firehole doors and shut off steam before applying the vacuum brake for our stop at Garstang.

Plate 10. 'Jubilee' Class, No.45689 *Ajax*, puts in some effort hauling a southbound freight over Brock Troughs on 18th August 1962. The M6 Motorway now parallels the railway at this location and where peace and quiet once was only interrupted momentarily by the passing of a train, now the incessant drone of passing traffic drowns all before it.
Photo, W.D.Cooper.

Plate 11. On 3rd August 1957 'Coronation' Pacific No.46248 *City of Leeds* passes Hest Bank with the Up Mid-Day Scot.
Photo, W.D.Cooper.

Now I could really take a rest for it was Jim's turn with the shovel while I leaned out of the window cleaning the wind deflector glass with a clean cloth out of my pocket and feeling like a top link fireman on the 'Caledonian'.

I really enjoyed the rest of our trip to Lancaster, leaning out of the cab watching the countryside flashing by as Jim struggled to get the coal into the box as I had earlier. He too got the hang of it before our Lancaster arrival. In the station we were relieved by Kevin and Paul so into the train we went for a nice cup of tea scrounged off Mick Sunter who kept quizzing us about what it was like with the shovel at speed, "Don't worry" we said, you will soon find out for yourself and with that no more was said on the subject. Approaching Hest Bank we closed the carriage window just in time as what appeared to be half a reservoir shot over our coach, "It looks like one of those two has done the same trick that I did,' I said to Jim, but he only smiled as Mick tried to find out what the joke was all about. At Oxenholme the last changeover took place and into the coach came Paul and Kevin, "God I nearly died when the scoop stuck at Hest Bank" said Paul. So now the cat was out of the bag but we all just laughed and shrugged it off. Each one of us tried the scoop that day and we all managed to get it stuck.

On arrival at Windermere Mick explained how he managed to completely miss the firehole near Kendal and covered Gilbert's polished boots with a few pounds of damp coal. Alan Pitcher fared no better as he soaked them all with dirty water from the slacking pipe whilst swilling the cab floor down. Our next job was to get rid of the coaching stock in one of the most unusual ways I have ever seen to this day.

Windermere is a terminus station and is situated on a steep downhill grade and the move was to uncouple the locomotive, pull the vacuum release cords on every coach and with the shunter in the brake van, push the stock up the bank over the points. The shunter now applied the handbrake and once the points were over and signal off, the locomotive dropped down to the turntable in order to be turned ready for the return journey South. By this time the points on the bank had been reversed, the shunter had released the handbrake to let gravity roll the train back into the station, stopping it again with the handbrake (How an accident never occurred during this manoeuvre is a total mystery). Once the locomotive had been turned it was taken onto the ashpit road and the tender filled with water from the column and the fire and ashpan cleaned. Now the locomotive's handbrake was applied and we departed into the porters cabin for a wash, a brew and a bite to eat.

During our break, Gilbert told us a tale about another fireman by the name of Tony Curtis (No not the film actor) who, a few months earlier, had worked the same train and on arrival at the ashpit had climbed onto the tender back to put the water bag into the tender filler hole. His driver had handed him the chain in order to let him pull the column arm over the filler hole. The column at Windermere worked on rollers, so you had to pull it uphill to get it over the hole and once the tender was full it would swing back to the drain instead of having to pull it back. Once over the filler hole, Tony asked his mate to turn the water on, to which the driver replied, "Make sure you lap the chain round the vent". Tony yelled back in his best voice "It s alright old boy I've got hold of it", so his mate with a knowing smile turned on the water and left him to it. Now once the force of the water arrived at the arm it started to pull the bag out of the filler hole and head back towards the drain. Tony tried in vain to keep it in place but not remembering to let go of the chain he was also dragged off the tender back and started to swing like Tarzan over the ash-pit, each too and fro movement brought him directly under the water gushing out of the pipe. He was totally soaked from this ordeal and decided to dry-out his clothes in the cab by draping them all over the firebox. The sight of Tony firing a Jubilee in nothing more than his underpants was a sight not to be missed, as some of the female passengers could confirm as they went as red as beetroots at this unusual sight. On hearing this tale we could hardly eat our sandwiches for laughing.

All to soon it was time to return to our locomotive with eyes still red from laughing so much.

Only Jim and myself returned to the engine with the driver and George, as we would be working her on the first leg to Oxenholme. Once aboard, Jim released the handbrake whilst I built up the fire and a matter of moments later the ground signal cleared and we proceeded to back onto our train. Alan Pitcher did the coupling up because he tended to have rather more difficulty than the rest of us the first time at Preston, so George demanded that he did it. This time he had no trouble with the task and had it tied on in a flash. At 1.20pm. the right away was given and *Aden* started her run home. Once on the bank with her seven coach train Gilbert opened her out as I closed the firehole doors and a column of jet black smoke shot from the chimney end into the overcast sky; the three cylinder beat sounded fantastic as *Aden* unleashed her power in the tree lined cutting. Now it was time to put on the injector to replenish the boiler and shoot about eight shovelfulls of coal around the firebox before our first booked stop at Staveley.

Following station duties we set off again accompanied by the fantastic sound from the front end as she got into her stride again and headed towards Burneside. From that point Jim took over the shovel for the rest of the climb to Kendal and Oxenholme where we got relieved by Kevin and Paul.

The rest of the trip was a repetition of the outward one apart from Mick Sunter getting the (Yes you guessed it) scoop stuck in the water troughs at Brock. On arrival at Preston the locomotive was uncoupled and we took her back on shed leaving her under the legs of the

Plate 12. Stanier Class 5, No.45343, departing Oxenholme with a Down parcels train on 29th June 1962. The branch to Windermere can be seen on the far right.
Photo, W.D.Cooper.

Plate 13. The scene at Carnforth on 15th June 1960, as Stanier Class 5 No.44778 departs with an Up passenger train on the W.C.M.L. Main line trains ceased to call at Carnforth from 1968.   Photo, W.D.Cooper.

massive coaling plant for the disposal men. On finishing duty that day, George told us all that for the rest of the week he would be taking us out on the road with different classes of locomotives varying from Black Fives to possibly a Princess Royal or Coronation class if one was on a morning turn to Crewe. What a memorable week that was, working freight and passenger turns to both Crewe and Carnforth but it did give us the knowledge of different methods of firing on the various types of engines. On the last day (Friday) we did get a chance to fire to Crewe on a Coronation but found the going too rough for our inexperienced bodies and more than once the Carlisle fireman had to take over to bring the boiler back up to working pressure.

The locomotive in question was No.46234 *Duchess of Abercorn*, not long out of Crewe works after an overhaul. The smell of new paint was very strong and the driver said it was a return running-in trip. We knew therefore that it could not be the locomotive at fault so it must have been down to us not firing her correctly. George told us not to worry as it was hard for everyone the first time on a 'Duchess' with their 50 square feet of grate area and 250 pounds per square inch of boiler pressure but we would soon get the hang of it with more practice on smaller locomotives in two weeks time.

CHAPTER FOUR
AMBITION REALISED

A cold winters morning in January 1961, saw the dawning of the day I had been looking to for so long. I was rostered to go for passing out as a fireman. I was met by a shortish gentleman who was Footplate Inspector, Arthur King. The first item on the agenda was a session in a classroom to find out what I knew about the job. This entailed answering questions about the locomotives injectors, firegrate, smokebox, the passage of steam and what seemed to be a thousand and one other questions on the technical working of the steam locomotive; not to mention the rule book and general working of trains, but after several hours he appeared to be satisfied with my answers. This was followed by a practical test on the mainline, working the 11.12 am. from Lancaster to Preston. This went quite smoothly and to make my day complete Arthur announced that I had indeed passed out as a Fireman.

However, passing out as a fireman did not mean that I would be going straight onto the locomotives every day, as I was now a passed cleaner, only getting a firing turn if a fireman called in sick or was on holiday. Most of my time was spent as a cleaner but at least I had gone another rung up the ladder in both my career and pay packet.

Some two weeks later I was busying myself shovelling spilled coal back into a wagon at the coaling plant when a driver appeared at my side. "Are you Bob Jackson" he inquired, "Yes" came my rapid reply as I wondered if something was wrong. "You're my fireman for the day as my mates gone sick". "What job is it", I nervously asked. "We're on the station pilot and don't worry because I know it's your first firing turn so I'll help you out the best that I can; now go and get your traps (bag, coat etc) and we'll get the other set of men relieved".

On the way to the station he introduced himself as Hughie McCann and we would get on fine together for the next seven hours or so. Our arrival at the south end of the station brought us into contact with our steed for the day. A grimy looking 3F, 0-6-0T, No.47360, more affectionately known as a "Jinty." The engine was standing in the short shunting neck awaiting it's next move.

The Fireman waiting to be relieved was Brian Townsend, accompanied by Driver Frank Thornton. Brian informed me that everything was O.K., and they had just topped up the water in the side tanks. Once aboard it was a totally different world for me as the space inside the cab was very restricted due to the size of the locomotive.

The fire inside the small firebox was banked up under the door and emitting a warm amber glow, the boiler pressure showing a respectable 140 Ibs per square inch (these engines had a working pressure of 160) and the boiler water level showing three quarters full. The first thing you notice in a cab so small is the huge reversing lever on a semi arched quadrant that takes up most of the drivers position on the right hand side, and the regulator handle fastened to the firebox backplate. This had to be handled by reaching over the top of the reversing lever, which made the driver stand at an awkward angle to operate it. From my side of the footplate you could see the fire-irons perched on top of the water side tank and the special short handled shovel needed on these engines propped by the side of the door. I had just managed to sit down on the small seat located on top of the tool cupboard when the ground disc signal came off with a loud 'clunk'. "The signal's come off Hughie", I shouted excitedly and wondered what to do next. "Right" he shouted back, "put on the steam brake, take the handbrake off and put one round of coal on the fire". This I did as the excitement mounted, knowing that I was now a true blue fireman for British Railways and this was my domain if only for the time being.

Once the handbrake was off Hughie took off the steam brake and pushed the reversing lever into full forward gear, opened the regulator about quarter of the way and with a loud hiss of escaping steam from the open cylinder drain cocks we began to move out of the shunting neck towards some parcels vans in the carriage sidings which were located between platforms 2 and 3. A few seconds later we buffered up to the vans where the shunter was waiting to couple us up. That job done we were ordered to take four of the vans out over Ribble bridge and come back behind a Carlisle bound parcels train that was due in platform 3 in five minutes time. Out over Ribble bridge we went at about 20-25mph with me getting carried away with the shovel until my mate reminded me we were not going to Wigan. "Take it easy" he said or we'll have an empty bunker. After those words I did tend to settle down and not get carried away again.

Three minutes after arriving behind the ground signal opposite Ribble Sidings Goods Yard I saw our train come round the bend at Skew Bridge hauled by 'Jubilee' No 45604 *Ceylon* with about 14 vans in tow. The drivers head was stuck out of the window as he kept a beady eye on the signal gantry guarding the Southern approaches to the station and braking the train at the same time.

As soon as he arrived in the platform our ground signal cleared and the 'Jinty' started to push the four vans over the points towards the signal gantry where the small subsidiary signal was pulled off to enable us to go behind the Carlisle parcels. Soon the shunter had uncoupled the vans onto the train and hooked us off the rear. "Right" shouted the shunter, "Go round to E.L. (East Lancashire) Carriage Sidings and bring out the Liverpool Exchange stock". "O.K." said Hughie and once the signal had been cleared by Preston No.1 box we proceeded back onto Ribble bridge then forward halfway down platform 7 behind another signal, and round a very sharp left hand bend onto the East Lancashire side of Preston Station.

Now we were under the control of East Lancashire box who soon had us in the carriage sidings on top of a five coach set of non-corridor stock that needed to be placed in number 10 platform. Once this shunt was completed we were told to return to the pilot sidings where we started from and have some lunch.

All that day we were kept busy in every nook and cranny around Preston station, in places with names like HORSE LANDING (With not a horse in sight), DARBY SIDINGS (Maybe that was where the horses were). BAKEHOUSE and PITT STREET to name a few. We even

Plate 14. On 19th April 1966, a view from the cab of 8F No.48714 working the 14.45pm Ribble Sidings-Garstang goods as Stanier Class 5, No.45120 passes Preston No.5 signal box. In the far background is the tall, elegant spire of St. Walburge's church which is located at Fylde Junction where the West Coast Main Line and the Fylde Coast routes diverge.

Photo, Mick Howarth.

ended up banking a heavy freight hauled by an Austerity from the Down Goods Line and up the short grade immediately north of the station to get him on his merry way to Carnforth.

Heavy freights often got stuck on this short but stiff pull and it was usually the station pilot that had to bank them out and I don't ever remember these little 'Jinties' failing the task once.

At about 2.30pm. we went to fill-up the water tank from the water column in the pilot sidings in readiness for our relief. This job alone took some stamina as first I had to climb up the locomotive to open the filler lid at the top front of the tank. Hughie then handed me the heavy chain that was fastened from the top of the column to the bottom of the thick leather hose bag. Now I had to lift the bag that was 18in wide and about 10ft long up on top of the tank and into the 12in diameter filler hole. If you didn't lay the hose along the top of the tank the bag would be forced out of the filler hole by water pressure. Once the bag was in place I gave a nod to Hughie who turned on the water by use of a large round wheel and gallons of water would rush into the tank as the bag began to pulsate with pressure. It was only necessary to fill up at one side as a connecting pipe went underneath the locomotive's boiler to the other tank and as water always finds its own level, both tanks are filled up at the same time.

A few minutes later we had full tanks and my mate turned off the water and I threw the bag out and closed the lid just as our relief arrived. Our relief was an old hand driver named Harry Preston who was restricted to the pilot links on medical grounds and his mate was another passed cleaner, Keith Hilton, (Nicknamed Stretch) who stood around 6ft 6in tall with less meat on him than a jockeys whip.

All that was required now was to return to the shed and book off duty at 3.30pm. Before leaving for home I noticed my name on the daily mark-out sheet, it just read "R.Jackson 3.30pm. DISP." Now that was a fresh one on me but at least I knew to report at eight o, clock the following morning. What they had in store for me was a complete mystery, so I asked Hughie what DISP was to which he replied, "you're on disposal duty knocking the fires out on the ash-pit but don't look so worried because you have a good mate, see if you can get hold of some old overalls to put over your own and keep them clean. Well I must be going" he said, "so good luck tomorrow" and with those words we went our separate ways.

Plate 15. The date is September 1964 as ex L&Y 'Crab' No.42925 waits for the off at Preston with what is probably the S.O. Fleetwood, Wyre Dock-Crewe fish train. Its a wonder the spotters above on the partly dismantled footbridge which once gave access to the Park Hotel, can stand the smell .

Photo, B.Magilton.

On arrival at home I sounded like a parrot as I excitedly told them all I had done on my first official firing turn and tomorrow I was getting another one. All they did was look at me with blank expressions and wondered if I needed a psychiatrist, but they soon became interested when I told them I was on higher pay. All I thought was they must have no soul at all.

The following morning I arrived at the shed at 7.40am. to make sure of being there before my driver signed on duty. Foreman Bill Robinson took one look and said he had never known such enthusiasm from a fireman rostered on a disposing turn. "Go in the messroom for a brew and I'll give you a shout when your driver turns up; oh and by the way your mates name is Andy Barton". At eight o' clock, a middle aged, good looking driver came into the messroom and asked, "Who is Bob Jackson?" "Me" I replied, "Are you Andy Barton?" "I sure am," he replied. "When you're ready make your way to the disposers cabin because I have some old overalls for you in there. Don't be too long though as there are two under the coaling tower now and we might as well get them done." To his astonishment I immediatly threw the rest of my tea down the sink, put the cup in my bag and followed him out of the door. In the disposers cabin I climbed into some dirty overalls that a rag and bone merchant would have turned his nose up at, but later I found out why they were perfect for the job. "Right' said Andy, "I'll do the first one and you just watch me".

His first job was to ring the foreman and tell him the locomotive number and in what direction it was facing (North or South), in this case it was a Black Five No.45398 facing north. "OK" said Bill, "it's for the 12.30pm. Barrow so leave it facing North." Andy then explained that if it wanted turning that would be the first job to do but in this case she was facing the right way.

Onto the footplate we climbed and the first thing he did was check the boiler water level in the gauge glass by opening the drain cock then closing it again, in order to watch the water return to it's own level. Next he released the handbrake, put it in forward gear, opened the ejector valve to release the vacuum brakes and slightly opened the regulator and the locomotive started to move towards the stop block. The idea was to run the locomotive a few yards over a set of spring loaded points that were permanently set for the coaling stage then reverse the locomotive in order to go back under the hopper. Once the tender was under the chute, Andy climbed onto the coal stage platform and into a small cabin that housed the controls to work the hopper. To operate the coal delivery apparatus the first thing to do was to push a large lever forward that directed the chute into the bunker space in the tender, followed by pressing a button that sent tons of coal crashing into the coal space. Soon the tender was full with about nine tons of best Yorkshire. Now the button was released and the lever returned to the central position ready for the next arrival. Andy made his way onto the footplate ready to move the locomotive back over the ash-pit and secured it.

It was now time to do the fire.This job entailed the use of a steel rake about 11ft long, a pair of firebar tongs with 6in grips and 5ft long handles,and a long dart shaped poker with an arrow

31

head to dig into the clinker and dislodge it. After putting on the blower his first task was to use the rake to push the good fire to the front end of the firebox and bare the firebars located at the back end of the box ready for removal. (If any clinker was on the bars he would have to use the dart to break it up). Once these bars were uncovered he removed the rake and put the tongs in the box to get hold of the first of four bars which had to be removed from the firegrate in order to provide a gap through which the fire needing to be removed could be raked into the ashpan. The idea was to get hold of one end of the bar, squeeze the long handles of the tongs together to get a firm grip on the bar lifting it from the grate and twisting it to the right at the same time in order to get it through the firehole and deposit it onto the footplate floor. Once the first one was out it was much easier to get at the other three for extraction. "Right." said Andy as he handed me the tongs, see if you can get the other three out but be ready when you pull them up as they tend to be heavy the first time you try it. As I lifted the first bar with the tongs the considerable weight tried to drag me through the firehole and into the firebox. With a titanic struggle I managed to accomplish this awkward task and drag the bar onto the footplate with arms that were beginning to feel like lead. The second one however proved even more difficult because it slipped away from the tongs and fell into the ashpan, as did the last one, so under the locomotive I had to go to pull them out and put them with the other two in the cab. "OK" said my mate, this is the tricky part, the idea is to clean all the back part of the grate of clinker and ash with the bent paddle and drop it all into the ashpan through the hole where the firebars have been removed, then use the rake to push it through the ashpan into the ash-pit. Next we have to rake back some live fire from the front of the box to the back, then rake all the front part into the hole in the same way as before and put some coal on the live fire under the door, replace the firebars and the fire is done.

Replacing the firebars was a work of art in itself as you had to balance the bar on the firehole lip-plate, get hold with the tongs and push it into the box without dropping it. Any ash on the holding bar could be scraped away by moving the firebar from side to side before installation. On removal, the rake would be glowing red hot and the asbestos gloves could not keep your hands from burning so a wad of rags was used as well, but even these started smouldering as your left hand started to slide down the rake handle as it was pulled from the box so the quicker it was removed and thrown out of the cab the better.

I once heard the tale of a fireman sliding the rake out through the cab door and shouting . "BELOW" but on release of the rake it didn't go with the usual clang as it hit the brick floor. On looking over the cab side all he saw was the ashpit cleaner flat on his back, knocked out cold. The lesson to learn was never to walk directly under the cab of a locomotive on the ash-pit. After cooling the rake down with water from a stand pipe I was told to take it underneath the locomotive and rake the rest of the ashes out of the ash-pan (If the wind was blowing in your direction it was advisable to tie a clean rag around your face as the ashes tended to stick to your sweating body like flies to a jam pot).

My next task was to get the firing shovel and empty the smokebox of black grit.(It was not soot) To open the smokebox door you had to turn the outer handle in an anti-clockwise direction to unscrew the lock, then turn the inner one a quarter of a tum the same way to unlock it. After cleaning out the smokebox it was also necessary to make sure that the smokebox ring was swept clean in order for the door to close with an airtight seal. If this was not done properly the door would allow air into the smokebox causing poor steaming and burning the door into the bargain. That job was soon done and in no time at all the smokebox was secured again. Now all that had to be done was to ring the foreman and ask him what road he wanted the locomotive on and leave it where ordered ready for the steam raiser, then go back and start on the next one in line.

Disposing was a dirty, Hot and laborious job but if you were lucky and both yourself and your mate got stuck into the job you could end up with an early finish. At Preston it was normal to do seven for a days work but a Coronation, Princess Royal or Britannia counted as two due to the size of the grate area (45-50sq ft). As well as being less laborious to work on, locomotives fitted with rocker grates and ashpans could be done in half the time, so these were always a welcome sight as they arrived on shed. Some locomotives were fitted with self cleaning smokeboxes, identifiable by a plate fitted to the smokebox door containing the letters "SC". These still needed cleaning out but not as often as locomotives without the fitting.

On the Friday of that week I was back on disposal duties but with another driver, Ronnie Gorton. We had just finished the fire on our first engine of the day, a Carlisle allocated Black Five, when Ernie Brown arrived in the disposers cabin (He was a restricted driver at the shed due to some ailment) to tell Ron he was being relieved for main line duties. So off to see the foreman Ron goes and leaves Ernie and myself to do the rest. We had just left the cabin to start on an ex L.N.W.R. G2a class 0-8-0, "Super D" when Alan Pitcher arrived on the scene to explain that I was also being relieved as the foreman wanted a word with me.

Arriving at the drivers lobby I was met by both the foreman (Joe Hughes) and Ronnie. I was asked by Joe if I could manage a main line turn as he had not got a spare fireman. He also explained that he was not in favour of this due to the fact that I had never been out on the main line before but Ronnie had said that he was willing to risk it because if that was Joe's attitude I would never get any main line experience. Within a matter of seconds it was agreed. On our way to the station I had all sorts of questions to ask Ron, "what sort of train is it? What class of locomotive. Where are we going and are we working back?" My mate tried his best to answer this barrage of questions, "The train we're working is 1T31, a pigeon special from Rugby to Carlisle, but I have no idea what our engine will be but it could be a Black Five. We'll find out if we are working back when we get there, but your first job when we get to the station is to make a brew in your can.

Once on the station I went to make the obligatory can of coffee and some five minutes later in came the train with what appeared a never ending string of parcel vans, and on the front, not a

Black Five, but a Jubilee, No.45730 *Ocean,* with the Crewe North shed code 5A on the smokebox door. She looked a bit rough externally but the Crewe fireman said she was steaming well and there was no problem at all. The boiler was showing three quarters full and a nice bed of fire on the grate that was built up at the back to the lip-plate; steam pressure was showing a healthy 225psi and the safety valves just starting to lift. Once the Crewe men had vacated the footplate all we wanted was a green flag from the guard to be on our way to the border city.

Some thirty seconds later the signal at the end of platform five was showing a clear road for the "Fast" line and I was looking back down the train for the tip off the guard. Soon his flag was waving above the heads of the passengers waiting for the next train in. "RIGHT AWAY", I shouted to Ron above the sound of the safety valves that had just erupted, sending steam shooting skywards. Ron gave a pop on the Stanier whistle and opened the regulator to full first valve. At first nothing appeared to happen except the blowing off had suddenly stopped due to the steam being taken from the boiler to the steam chest, then the massive 6ft-9in driving wheels started to move as 45730 began to get the train out of town on the 90 mile leg of it's journey to Carlisle.

After passing under Fishergate bridge located just north of Preston station, I fired about ten rounds of coal into the fire-box, closed the fire-hole doors and a column of black smoke shot

Plate 16. Class 5, No.44674, passes beneath the magnificent array of signals north of Preston station with the 10.55am. Preston-Blackpool Central in September 1964.   Photo, J.A.Oldfield.

skywards accompanied by the beautiful sound of the distinctive muffled three cylinder beat as we headed towards the massive signal gantry containing 29 semaphore arms that controlled the lines which radiated to Blackpool, Carlisle, the Deepdale branch, and the shed roads. I once heard the tale of a Manchester driver who had mistakenly taken the small left hand signal for the shed road as the calling on arm for the slow line to Blackpool and ended up under the coaling tower with a full passenger train (How he ever explained that I will never know). All went well until passing Oxheys Cattle Dock when my mate put on the blower, opened the firehole doors and slammed the regulator shut before applying the vacuum brake. At that moment she started to blow off again so I operated the exhaust steam injector to top up the boiler and keep her quiet before going to see what the matter was.

On arriving at Ron's side of the cab I could see the starter signal offbut the distant was on for Barton & Broughton. On the approach to his outer home signal the small left hand signal came off to take us into the long passing loop. "We must have an express behind us" Ron explained, so as we arrived at the home signal I got onto the telephone to the signalman who informed me that we would be following the Birmingham - Glasgow express which was now out of Preston, and hard on our heels. I relayed these instructions to my mate before going back to my side of the footplate in order to watch the express pass by. I had just made it when the train approached, going like the clappers in a flurry of smoke and steam. At the head of the 16 bogies was the last member of the Coronation Class Pacifics, No.46257, *City of Salford* and what a majestic sight she was with her maroon livery glinting in the sun. Following the passage of the express the points went over and our signal came off to take us back out of the loop and onto the main line.

My next problem came a few minutes later at Brock when I had just finished building up the fire, "WATER TROUGHS" Ron shouted, OH NO I thought, thinking of my earlier escapade with Gilbert and George as I went over to the other side of the cab, "NOW" yelled my mate as I screwed the scoop into the trough but this time I kept my eyes on the tender gauge and as soon as the pointer was showing almost 4000gals I started to take the scoop out and not a drop came in the cab.

All went well as we reeled off the miles passing Garstang & Catterall, Bay Horse, Oubeck, Lancaster, Hest Bank (Another top-up from the troughs) Bolton-le-Sands and Carnforth. On the approach to Hincaster Junction my mate started to blow on the whistle to inform the signalman that we needed a banker from Oxenholme to the top of Grayrigg Bank, and once we were clear the points at Oxenholme the train was stopped until a 2-6-4 tank engine came on to our rear. After buffering up, the banker gave two crows and Ron whistled back and opened the regulator to start the arduous climb of the first of the two steep banks on the West Coast line to Carlisle.

In the time we had been stopped I had built up the fire again with a thick bed of coal and as we started away I closed the firehole doors leaving the live steam injector on and the boiler topped up with bursts from the exhaust injector. Passing Peat Lane, the exhaust looked like a dark cloud as a column of black smoke shot high in the cutting only to mingle with the smoke of the banker a few seconds later.

By this time my arms were beginning to feel like lead as I had to start firing again and sweat was running down my back like a river. On past Hay Fell and Lambrigg Crossing we went and I was grateful to see the top of Grayrigg where the banker dropped off as we descended down the gradient past Low Gill where Ron once again whistled for a banker at Tebay to assist us up

Plate 17. Passing the now vanished Garstang & Catterall Station heading north with a train of Covhop wagons is B.R Standard 9F, 2-10-0 No.92165. This locomotive is one of the class fitted with a double chimney to improve their steaming capabilities, and a mechanical stoker for working the Water Orton-Carlisle freight turns from Saltley depot.   Photo, Mick Howarth.

the 1 in 75 bank to Shap Summit (91 6ft above sea level).

On the approach to Tebay the distant signal was on but I tried to get as much water out of Dillicar troughs as possible whilst my mate was braking the train for the outer home signal. For this second time we were put into a passing loop to let another express pass us, this one had a Royal Scot 4-6-0, No.46166 *London Rifle Brigade* at it's head but hauling only seven coaches did not require a banker and shot through Tebay at a fair clip on it's way to Carlisle.

Whilst waiting for the express to pass I was busy raking some of the depleted coal supply forward in the tender with the coal pick as Ron was building up the fire for me and as I came

Plate 18. 2-6-4T, No.42110, gives assistance to 'Britannia' No.70028 *Royal Star*, seen approaching Shap summit on 30th April 1968.   Photo, W.D.Cooper.

out of the tender there was a nice thick bed of coal on the fire burning through nicely and the boiler three quarters full of water plus 220psi of steam.

Now it was our turn; the points went over, the signal came off and Ron moved the train out onto the main line and stopped once the train was clear of the junction to allow the banker to come off Tebay shed and buffer up behind. On this occasion it was a Standard Class 4 of the 75xxx series that had the job of helping us to the summit. Following the usual whistles, Ron opened the regulator to full first valve with the reverser in full forward gear as we felt the banker start to push.

During our slow acceleration up the bank the reverser was screwed back to 50% and the regulator opened up to full second valve and the exhaust crashed out in a crescendo as the Jubilee responded to everything asked of it. I worked the exhaust injector to keep the boiler water topped up. (The live steam has been on all the time from Tebay) After passing Scout Green and Shap Wells we ran over the summit as the banker dropped off to head back down to Tebay Shed and await it's next call of duty. For us it was now all downhill and I had a chance to rest my aching limbs as we ran effortlessly through Thrimby, Bessie Ghyll, Penrith, Plumpton and Wrea to Carlisle.

Plate 19. North of Shap Summit was the small Shap station. On 6th November 1964, Class 5, No45363 passes tender first with a train of stone hoppers.

Photo, J.A.Oldfield.

Plate 20. On a fine summers day in 1964, rebuilt 'Patriot' No.45531 *Sir Frederick Harrison* is seen passing Scout Green with a mixed freight.

Photo, W.D.Cooper.

On our arrival at Carlisle we were ordered to take the loop to Upperby Shed located just South of the station as the station pilot was taking the vans away to liberate the pigeons. On arrival at the shed we left 45730 in the capable hands of the disposing crew and headed into the messroom for a well earned brew and a bite to eat. We had just completed our lunch when the Shed Foreman came in and asked for the Preston men off lT31. Ron went to see him and came back saying we are working back to Preston assisting the 'Mid-Day Scot' with a Midland class 2P tender engine that was wanted back down South. I had never been on one of these locomotives but knew they were noted for their fast running with 6ft 9in driving wheels although weak on power. With only two cylinders and a boiler pressure of 180psi they usually only ran about with 4 coaches on their own.

The engine in question was already prepared in the roundhouse so all was needed was to spread the fire, take off the handbrake and drop down to the ringing out point.

Once off the shed we proceeded tender first into one of the middle roads at Citadel station on top of a Coronation Pacific No.46243 *City of Lancaster.* "Right hook us on to that" said Ron, so in between I went and coupled up, took his lamp off the front and ours off the tender back, gave him his lamp and arranged ours at the front as one over each buffer to denote express passenger train. I was just doing this when the Carlisle fireman came up with the headboard 'The Mid-Day Scot' and placed it on our smokebox bracket. All we had to do now was to await the arrival of the train from Glasgow Central. Some eight minutes later in it came hauled by Coronation No. 46224 *Princess Alexandra* which was being detatched. Soon the incoming engine was hooked off and on it's way to Upperby shed as our signal came off to take us both out behind the ground signal and back onto the train. Following the hooking on procedure by the Carlisle fireman, the guard arrived to give both my mate and the Carlisle driver the train loading of 17 bogies. On departure our little Class 2 was the first to give a beat, followed almost immediately by an enormous "WOOSH" from the double blastpipes of the Coronation. This made me shoot round like a bullet and due to the low Fowler tender all I could see was a gigantic smokebox flanked either side with massive smoke deflectors and all hell erupting from the chimney end; scared!, I thought she was going to run clean over us.

Soon we passed Upperby shed and started the assault on the bank towards Penrith and Shap Summit. The racket from the Coronation's exhaust was absolutely deafening on our footplate as I tried my best to keep the boiler pressure up on the Class 2 but I am sure the train engine was pushing us as well as pulling the train. The Carlisle fireman looked out of his cab and gave me a sign as to get out of the way, but only as a joke of course. Once over Shap Summit the speed built up at an alarming rate as we shot past Scout Green and Tebay but now the going was easier on the downhill grade and on arrival at Preston we were relieved by a set of Crewe men who were working the train forward.

That trip really gave a boost to my ego but for the following weeks it was back to the more mundane tasks of both cleaning and firing on both pilots and local trip workings.

Plate 21. At Carlisle, the London Midland Region shared lines with the Eastern. A4, No.60031 *Golden Plover* is seen alongside Carlisle No4 box with an Edinburgh, Waverley-Carlisle train on 18th April 1965.

Photo, J.A.Oldfield.

Plate 22. With name-plates removed, an ex Eastern Region Britannia preserves its anonyminity after arrival at Carlisle in September 1967.

Photo, D.Hill.

One of the trippers was on the dock branch, where Preston based G2As 'Super 'D's' worked the coal and banana trains between the docks and Bamber Bridge Yard, some four or five miles away. The dock branch itself was quite a sight as it descended down a 1 in 29~then I in 33 bank from a point south of the station, over Strand Road by an ungated level crossing and onto the dock estate. More than once these trains have run away, with the driver blowing hard on the whistle for the dock police to stop the traffic going along Strand Road as he would not be able to pull up at the signal protecting the crossing. Working from the docks and up the bank could be even more spectacular as the drivers had to take a flying run, flat out from well inside the the docks. Once the traffic had been stopped, the signal to leave would be given and the train would accelerate with the 'Super D' straining to build up as much speed as possible before crossing over the road and onto this awsome bank, which as well as the grade contained two tunnels. From the firemans side it was a very daunting task as you had to have a full head of steam with the minimum of water in the boiler as once you hit the bank (Smokebox First) all the boiler water would rush and concentrate over the firebox. If the boiler was three quarters full on the level, once you got into the bank the locomotive would start to prime which meant it had a good chance of applying the brakes.

Plate 23. Inside Preston Shed, August 1963, as a pair of L&NW 2-8-0 Super D's sleep. This class were often used to work the Preston Dock branch trains.

Photo, D.Hill.

On approaching the summit you had to put the injectors on to stop the lead plugs from fusing and failing the locomotive. Another of the fireman's tasks was to pick-up the single line token from a spring loaded mechanism attached to a post as you came off the dock estate and hand it to the signalman at Preston No.1A signalbox, (Going the other way you picked it up from the signalman and handed it to the traffic police on Strand Road). The token holder contained a large loop acting as it's handle so as you passed the holder you could put your arm through it and drag it out of it's mechanism. I heard the tale one day of one of the firemen missing the loop altogether, somehow managing to get his arm around the mechanism and took the lot out of the post.

Plate 24. Preston No.1A signal box where the single line token for the Dock Branch was obtained/handed in, photographed about 1966.

Photo, P.Hampson.

Another incident that comes to mind was the messroom story of a cyclist that just beat the train over the crossing but as the "Super D" went over a piece of red hot cinder from the chimney went into his hair and he was last seen riding along Strand Road with his head on fire The other working on the dock branch was a banker as all the heavy coal empties and loaded banana trains had to be banked from the dock up to Preston N.U. If the fireman on the front locomotive missed the single line token altogether the train engine driver could give a blow on the whistle and the bank engine fireman would pick it up. Not long after I started working on these jobs, the Super D's became redundant and the working were taken over by 350hp diesel shunters that performed the task very well. However, the sight and sound of the old Super D's will never be forgotten as they blasted their way off the docks.

One bitterly cold day I was working the local 15 target that picked up and set down freight in and out of the small yards around Farington, Lostock Hall, Todd Lane Junction and Leyland. About 11.30am. we arrived in Lostock Hall gas works with our Super D, and following the shunting of the wagons decided it was time for a bite and a brew. My driver for that day was Arthur Duxbury with Gordon Jackson (No relation) acting as the guard. Following our break, Gordon explained that he was having trouble with the stove in the brakevan as it was not drawing air and the van was like a fridge, "no problem" said Arthur, "the flue must be blocked and the only way to shift it is to put a couple of detonators on the fire and close the door." Off the guard went to carry out the task but instead of using two detonators he put on four or five, and closing the door he climbed onto the roof with a shunting pole, proceeding to ram the pole down the flue with a great amount of gusto. A matter of seconds later the detonators exploded in the stove with an almighty 'BANG' that blew off the door and sent a spout of soot up the flue that completely covered Gordons face. How it failed to blow him off the roof I will never know but he never did that trick again.

One of my favourite local freight jobs was the morning turn from Ribble Sidings to Pilling on the ex Garstang and Knott End Railway known to everyone as the "Pilling Pig". This trainsfirst port of call from Preston was Garstang & Catterall with wood pulp for the local mill and usually the tonnage was very high to that point. Sometimes even having to be double headed to Garstang with the assisting locomotive returning back later light engine to Preston. From Catterall the train went down the tokenless single line to Pilling but the next call was at Garstang Town where the old passenger station was still intact, although the line had been closed to passenger trains for many years and the only train now using it was the 'pilling Pig'.

Plate 25. Two B.R. Standard types, 'Britannia' No.70016, minus its *Ariel* nameplates, and 2-10-0, No.92021 are seen at Garstang & Catterall Station on 23rd June 1966.   Photo, W.D.Cooper.

There always seemed to be some incident with this train and one wet Monday morning was no exception. The driver in question was an old hand by the name of Jas Harrison, noted for his heavy working of any locomotive he was driving.

On this particular day we had a Black Five No.45382, and once clear of Catterall Yard he shot off like a bat out of hell on the down gradient towards Garstang Town station. On applying the brakes for our stop, the wheels locked and she started to slide on the greasy rails and even with the application of sand the slide continued. He even tried alerting the guard to apply the brake in his van but was unable to raise his attention. By this time we were approaching the station at about 35mph and had no hope of stopping. Located just beyond the station by a matter of yards were a set of wooden level crossing gates that were normally opened to the railway by the fireman while the guard sorted out his train. Not on this day though, for in no time at all the gates were reduced to nothing more than a pile of firewood as 45382 slid straight through them.

Following our shunting of the coal wagons we proceeded on our way through Nateby and Omo Crossing to Pilling, where once again we shunted the loaded coal wagons in and the empties out before stopping for lunch. During our break, Jas went onto the phone to report the earlier incident at Garstang Town.(And no doubt say he was sorry accompanied by a bit of grovelling).

The return trip with the empties had to be tender first all the way back to Preston's Ribble Sidings, with just one stop at Catterall and on a wet day like this was very uncomfortable as all the rain came into the cab soaking the crew from head to foot. Tuesday morning saw me on the same working, with the same driver, same locomotive (45382) and the same guard. One notable thing was we didn't require double heading as the train was fairly lightly loaded and following our shunting at Catterall Jas set off again in his usual manner. At that moment it was dry but it had been raining up to twenty minutes earlier, whilst braking coming down the bank the locomotive decided once again to do a dance and put the fear of God in poor Jas. As we rounded the curve through Town station the first thing I saw was two painters putting the last lick of paint on some brand new crossing gates, I gave the whistle a hefty blow as the painters jumped clear just before Jas repeated the previous days performance and demolished these as well. "Sorry lads, bad rail" was all he could say on the matter. I was later told that one daywhilst working a local passenger train from Preston to Southport he demolished one half of a set of double gates worked by a signalbox and on the return trip he hit the other half (At least he was consistent).

For the next couple of months I worked a variety of trains, varying from freights to Warrington, Heysham, Carnforth and Crewe, to passenger and parcels workings to Barrow, Manchester, Liverpool, Crewe and Carlisle with a mixture of locomotives ranging from Class Eights and Austerities to Black Fives, Britannias and Royal Scots. But a dark cloud was looming on the horizon when week later we received notice that Preston shed (24K) was to

44

close on the 11th September 1961 and if no preference was given for another depot the men would be transferred along with the work to nearby Lostock Hall shed that was located just a couple of miles southeast of Preston.

As I still lived in Coppull with no personal transport of my own I decided to transfer to Newton Heath in Manchester because I had at least a train service from either nearby Chorley or Wigan, So I filled the form out with an 8C move back to Preston at the earliest opportunity.

Although Preston shed itself had closed a signing on point was retained for sets of men to sign on in order to relieve crews arriving at Preston. An 8C move allowed men transferred away on the closure of the shed to return as soon as a suitable vacancy occurred at the home signing on point.

Plate 26 The 2.40pm. Pilling to Preston goods known locally as the 'Pilling Pig' is photographed departing Pilling on 23rd March 1962, headed by 'Black Five' 4-6-0 No.45388. The Garstang & Knott End Railway closed to passengers in 1930 but remained open to goods traffic as far as Pilling until complete closure in 1965. Driver George Beardswood and the Author look out for the camera. Photo, Ron Herbert.

Plate 27 One of the early batch of 'Black Five' 4-6-0's No.45017 is seen on number 8 road at Lostock Hall MPD on 22nd March 1963, photographed from the sand drying plant.   Photo, Mick Howarth.

Plate 28. Also seen at Lostock Hall, on number 10 road in 1962, one of the last 'Patriots' to remain in service, No.45505 *The Royal Army Ordnance Corps.*   Photo, Paul Tuson.

CHAPTER FIVE
FIRING ON THE LANKY

On Monday, September 11th 1961, I duly arrived for my first day at Newton Heath shed, Manchester, and what a contrast it was to Preston; instead of the nine inside roads and two outside, I was now confronted with a shed of twenty four through roads plus at least six outside ones. You could have fit Preston shed into one corner of it. The shed was situated in the middle of the fork where the line to Oldham swung away to the right and the one to Rochdale to the left. Inside was a huge amenity block that even included showers and a fully equipped canteen neither of which had graced Preston Shed; Newton Heath was the largest shed on the ex-Lancashire and Yorkshire railway. The shed still survives today but is now a diesel multiple unit maintenance depot for North West Trains and is only a shell of it's former self compared to how it was in the days of steam.

When I arrived I was still only a passed cleaner but was firing every day on many different kinds of work. To get me started I was rostered in the disposal link with a pleasant driver named Andy Courtley. From the beginning we got on like two peas in a pod as he wanted to know all about the workings at Preston and I about this depot. He explained that the most coveted workings were the 9.30am. passenger to Glasgow (As I used to observe from Cowling Mill) and a freight from Moston Yard to Camden, (London) where the men booked off. The biggest bulk of the work however, consisted of the Manchester to Blackpool and Southport trains. They also had other workings to York, Oldham, Wigan, Leeds, and Rochdale, plus many freights to places like Healey Mills and the bank engines that assisted heavy goods trains up Miles Platting Bank.

We had been disposing for a couple of weeks on all different types of locomotives such as 2-6-4 tanks, Crabs, Class 8's, Black 5's, Jubilee's, Scots and Britannias, when one Wednesday morning, just as we had finished disposing of an Austerity, a 'Super D' arrived at the coaling tower having worked in with a train from Wigan. There were always three sets of disposal men working in turn, as and when the locomotives arrived, so the 'Super D' was allocated to the next set up.

The crew in question, Bert Simmester and his Fireman went to sort it out but came back into the cabin a very short while later saying they were willing to give this one up if anyone was willing to do it. "Why don't we do it?" I said to Andy. "I'm used to those engines as we had our own at Preston". "Go and check the boiler water level first" he replied. On trying the test cock all I could see were air bubbles indicating that the boiler was bunged up to the whistle.

Now when these engines were full to the brim anyone trying to move it was in for a nasty shock because once the regulator was opened it was impossible to close it again due to the pressure of water on the regulator valve. I went back into the cabin to tell my mate. "We're not doing it" he said. Bert tried another trick, "How about if we do the fire and you shed it, seeing you have a 'Wessy' fireman." "Not a hope" replied Andy "so it's your problem now" (The other set had also refused). Once fire cleaning had been completed all locomotives were taken via the left hand side of the shed, down to the far end and onto the turntable whether they required turning or not, in order for the points to be set for any one of the shed roads. When the 'D's' fire was completed a very nervous Bert climbed aboard, took off the handbrake, released the brakes and gingerly pulled down on the regulator. As soon as it started to move he tried to close it again but as expected it stuck open. Bert was soon going like the clappers and screaming his head off going past the side of the shed. A matter of seconds after passing from sight, all we heard was the almighty crash as the 'D' ran into the turntable well. Luckily Bert was not harmed except for a bruised knee when he jumped off the footplate, but it took the breakdown gang and steam crane a good couple of hours to extract the engine out of the well and repair the damaged turntable.

Some six weeks later I was promoted out of the disposal link and up into the York link. The work in the latter was wide and varied, not just working to York as the name suggests, for we also had jobs to Blackpool, Southport, Leeds and Oldham, to name just a few. My driver in this link was Stan Booth who was also the Union Branch Secretary at the shed. He was in his mid-forties and had a very nice character, but our third trip together almost ruined everything. Luckily however, we ended it up laughing it off.

This particular Saturday we booked on duty at 12.40pm. to prepare our own engine, take it light to Manchester Victoria and work the 1.48pm. parcels train to Leeds, returning as passengers on the first available return service. Our locomotive for the trip was Stanier Class 5, No. 44890, that stood on number 12 road in the shed.

During our preparation of the Black Five I remembered that I had put a large tin of baked beans in my haversack which would do very nicely for my lunch. I decided to place the tin of beans on top of the hot manifold pipe and wedge it in place with two pieces of coal.

All went well as we rang off shed, and on arrival at Victoria Station we coupled up to the seven or eight vans that stood in platform 14. We were booked to stop at Stalybridge, Huddersfield, Dewsbury and Leeds, where we were to be relieved by a set of Holbeck men.

We departed Manchester some three or four minutes late due to awaiting some parcels off another incoming train, but Stan was determined to get to Leeds early in order to catch an earlier than booked train back. Soon we were up Miles Platting Bank and took the right hand signal to take us through Park Station, Droylesden and on to Diggle.

After passing Diggle box we suddenly shot into the inky blackness of Standedge Tunnel that separates Lancashire from Yorkshire. Some three quarters way through the tunnel there was an almighty 'Bang' in the cab, so Stan thinking the gauge glass had broken threw his coat over the left hand boiler water gauge and I did the same over the right one, and we both operated the shut off cocks at the same time. "I THINK I'VE BEEN HIT!" he yelled, "ME TOO" I shouted back, "and I think I'm bleeding" I added. "Well we can't do anything until we get out of this damn tunnel so just sit down and wait" Running through that tunnel seemed like a lifetime in the smoky darkness.

At long last the locomotive ran over the clapper-board by the signal that warned us of the tunnel end, so back into the daylight we ran. Once our eyes had adjusted to the glare I took one look at Stan as he did the same to me, my first impression was that Stan had contracted measles as his face was full of red blotches but on looking around the cab it was evident that he had not caught any virus because the whole of the footplate, including the tender front, cab roof and firebox backplate were covered in baked beans and what I thought was blood was in fact tomato sauce. "You did put a hole in the top of that tin didn't you?" he asked, "No' I replied, "What do you need a hole in it for?" "To stop it from — never mind" he said, "IDIOT" was the last word he said as we removed our coats and reset the water cocks.

On arrival at Huddersfield, the Station Inspector, on seeing Stan's face, came rushing up to locomotive and asked, "Have you had an accident?" "Don't ask" was the only answer he got

Plate 29. Photographed at Newton Heath Shed in April 1961, ex Lancashire & Yorkshire 0-6-0 No.52271, keeps company with sister engine No.52207. The Author transferred to this shed in 1961 after Preston shed closed.

Photo, Paul Tuson.

and I was ordered to wash down the whole of the footplate with the degging pipe while Stan went to wash his face.

Returning from Leeds in the train, my mate suddenly burst out in a fit of laughter as the rest of the passengers in the compartment wondered what the joke was all about. My last comment on the subject was to ask Stan, "How do they manage to cram so many beans in a tin?" But that only started another outburst of hysterics. Many years later in diesel days when I was back at Preston, I was sat one day in the traincrew messroom having a brew and a bite when in walked Stan after working in with a class 47 and on seeing him I asked, "Do you want a spoonful of beans Stan?" "I've never eaten beans since 1961" he said, as all the other men wondered what it was all about. Well now they know:

My time at Newton Heath was now coming to an end as I was soon to be ordered back to Preston as a booked fireman (I had completed my needed 270 firing turns just before the baked beans special). One of my most cherished trips with Stan came just three working days before my return to Preston which was to take place on 12th March 1962. So much so that I was asked originally to write an article on it by Mick Howarth, then editor of "Northern Railways" magazine and later reproduced it again for the Stanier Locomotive Society Limited of the Severn Valley Railway for inclusion in their Spring 1986 issue of their magazine "Black Eight," so I think it is only fair to reproduce it one more time for those who did not read the original.

The article in original form was entitled "Firing *Dauntless*" and this part I dedicate to Stan.

Turning the clock back to 6th March 1962, we will take a trip down memory lane by reminiscing about a firing turn from Manchester Victoria to York via Huddersfield and Leeds with 'Jubilee' 4-6-0, No.45717 *Dauntless.*

At 8.20am, I reported for duty at Newton Heath Depot to be greeted by my driver. I had fired for Stan on the same turn only two weeks previously so I knew his driving technique with the 5X, as he knew mine from the other side of the cab. After collecting our workings and drivers ticket we made our way to Dean Lane Station to catch the local service to Manchester Victoria. Upon arrival at our destination we made our way to the porters room in order to make our first brew of the day before trotting over to platform 16 in order to relieve the Liverpool men who had brought in the Newcastle train from Lime Street. The train had arrived on time with well used 45717 at the front and a quick word with the "Scouse" fireman led me to believe that the old girl had lost none of her sparkle since her last visit to Crewe works. The only cloud on the horizon was the Fowler tender with which *Dauntless* was paired, I never did like these tenders on a passenger locomotive but there was nothing I could do about it, so I began to build up the fire ready to do battle with Miles Platting Bank.

At 10.15 the colour light signal flickered to green as the safety valves began to lift, the guard waved his flag, and with a huge upward pull on the regulator Stan got us moving. *Dauntless* however decided it was time to slip and with a roar from the chimney end tried to lift the roof off Victoria Station. My mate had been ready for her and shut off steam and applied the sanders before re-opening the regulator. With the familiar "Jubilee" muffled three cylinder beat, 45717 blasted over East Junction past the modern signalbox and started the assault of Miles Platting Bank.

Once clear of the junction, Stan screwed back the reverser a couple of turns and pushed the regulator all the way home in the horizontal position. The exhaust crashed out in a loud crescendo as I tried my utmost to keep the hungry fire supplied with coal and sufficient water in the boiler by keeping on the live steam injector, supplemented by bursts from the exhaust injector. Soon Stan shut off steam for the 20mph curve at Miles Platting where we leave the line to Oldham and swing right towards Phillips Park. Once clear of the restriction ,the cut-off is screwed back to 50% and the regulator resumes the wide open horizontal position. With this treatment *Dauntless* unleashes her power passing Park Station to the entertainment of passengers awaiting the local back to Victoria.

With all signals showing "Right Away" the beat intensified as we shot through Clayton Bridge and Droylesden. On the approach to Ashton station my mate opened the firehole doors, put on the blower and shut off steam to let her coast through the series of bridges and tunnels towards our first stop at Stalybridge. Following station duties that lasted only a couple of minutes which also gave me just enough time to build up the fire, the guard decided it was time to leave, so after a pop on the whistle Stan took control of the Bank Hall locomotive and opened the regulator to full first valve.

As we pounded into Stalybridge Tunnel it felt as if all the air had been drawn out of my lungs to be replaced by acrid fumes and steam from the locomotive's boiler. Emerging from the tunnel found both Stan and I leaning over the cab sides to drink in the beautiful fresh air as the smoke continued to swirl around inside the cab. Out in the open *Dauntless* started the long

Plate 30. A Liverpool Lime Street-Newcastle express hauled by re-built 'Patriot' No.45534, *E.Tootal Broadhurst* ,passing Droylsden on 18th May 1958.   Photo, B.Hilton.

climb to Standedge Tunnel, and passing Mossley was in full cry with 55% cut-off and full regulator. Speed barely reached 50mph up the bank with our nine coach load. Once passed Greenfield my mate prepared to shut off steam in order to let her run down to 40mph on the entrance to Standedge Tunnel and two minutes later we shot into the eerie blackness on our way to Yorkshire. Talk about the black hole of Calcutta, it's not a patch on Standedge Tunnel on a spring morning, and as we ran into it the only thing to be seen was the glare of the firebox.

About a quarter way through we passed another express on it's way to Manchester hauled by a 'Black Five' and all the exhaust from that completely filled the tunnel which added to the fumes from *Dauntless* and made Stan's job a lot harder as he tried to sight the exit warning light.

After what seemed like ages we approached the clapper-board adjacent to the warning light and with a "rat-a-tat-tat" the locomotive wheels passed over the clapper-board giving Stan the signal to shut the regulator allowing us to coast out of the tunnel and through the first station over the Yorkshire border at Marsden.

From Marsden to Huddersfield the run is all downhill which gave me a chance to top-up the boiler and take a breather by leaning on the window arm rest to wipe the well cleaned wind deflector glass, this must have been the most polished item on a steam locomotive. It was a very welcome break indeed to lean out of the window and feel the cold air cooling my now sweating face.

The route down through Slaithwaite and Longwood goods took us into the first of two tunnels located on the approach to Huddersfield with Stan concentrating on his braking ready for our station stop.

Stopping with the tender alongside the water column I clambered up and "put the bag in" to top up our depleted water supply as the station staff looked after the passengers. A couple of minutes later saw our water supply replenished, the passengers boarded and a green signal showing. The guard waved his flag and with a pop on the whistle *Dauntless* eased the train over the maze of points and out onto the large viaduct.

As soon as we were clear of the station area Stan screwed back the cut-off to 50% and pushed the regulator up to the customary horizontal position which is a signal for me to get stuck into the fire again. After letting *Dauntless* have five rounds of coal into the box I closed the doors and a column of black smoke erupted from the chimney end. Five miles further on we rushed through Mirfield and Ravensthorpe before running into Dewsbury where I had time to swill down the footplate with the degging pipe and dampen down the coal at the same time. By the time we departed, the footplate was looking clean and tidy, and smelling a little fresher. It was always a fascination to me to watch the steam rising from the wet floorboards to be dragged into the firehole by the draught created by the exhaust blast.

There are numerous curves from Dewsbury to Leeds and all Stan's time was taken up by looking out for the distant signals while I began again to feed the hungry firebox witnessed by another show of black smoke from the chimney end. I was just getting ready to start firing again when my mate popped his head in and shouted that the fire would do to Leeds as we were now on the outskirts and would be arriving shortly and true enough, in a few minutes the two tracks opened out into the massive junction approaching Leeds City Station.

Whilst stood in the station and topping up the tender water from the handy column,it gave me time to study the mixed bag of ex-LMS and LNER locomotives that thronged the platform and through lines. These ranged from Black Fives, Jubilees and Royal Scots, to B1, A2 and A3 classes, not to mention the B.R. Standards and Austerities that were serviced at nearby Holbeck and Neville Hill Depots. Just as I was getting engrossed by this spectacle, Stan turned off the water supply and shouted "chuck the bag out Bob, it's time to go."

All the time I had been up on the tender my mate had been "gassing her up" and when I climbed back on the footplate there was an abundance of fresh coal in the box burning throughnicely; this gave me another chance for a rest as Stan received the "right away" Now it was time for *Dauntless* to show the LNER what she was made of, and once clear of the station limits, Stan opened her up. Passing the goods yards she was showing her paces as the speed increased at a rapid rate.

Four miles out from Leeds we thundered through Cross Gates Station at an almost alarming rate, the passengers waiting on the platform realised that this could not be their stopping train to Hull and all stood back. All that is, except one elderly gentleman, who absolutely refused to

Plate 31. The 5pm Liverpool Lime Street-Newcastle is seen departing Huddersfield about 1961. This working was diagramed for a single engine load but on this occasion 'Royal Scot' No.46127 *Old Contemptibles* gives assistance to 'Jubilee' No.45563 *Australia..*   Photo, Jim Carter.

budge. As we tore through the platform we saw his feathered trilby hat flying up into the air with the owner in hot pursuit, my mate commented "I reckon that will teach him not to be too clever, what do you think?" "Quite right" I replied as I started to build up the fire again All went well as we passed through Garforth and Mickelfield with the 5XP performing fantastically. I was now starting to ache all over and sweating profusely, but would Stan ease up would he ....?

Soon we approached Church Fenton where the lines opened up from double to quadruple track as we joined the route from Wakefield and Sheffield. "This is where the fun began as I shouted to Stan, "looks like there's an Eastern express coming up on the other road." He yelled back "how far away is he?" and I replied "quite away but closing fast." "Right, get the old girl hot, I'm going to give him a run for his money." And with that, Stan opened the regulator to full and dropped the cut-off down no less than 55% and *Dauntless* began to respond. After giving her two dozen shovelfulls around the box and closing the doors, I operated the exhaust steam injector to keep the boiler water three quarters full, (The live steam injector had been on all the time) this left me with time to see how she would perform coupled with Stan's expertise as an engineman. Looking back, I told my mate that the A3 was still gaining on us but at a much reduced rate. At this moment the driver of the Eastern express must have twigged what was going on and took up the challenge. The exhaust of the approaching A3 shot high into the air in a black column. "He's seen us" I shouted as the adrenaline rushed through my now rested body. 45717 s speed was now well up into the eighties and the connecting rods were just a blur as she took this terrible pounding, the cab almost rattling to pieces. Moments later the A3, No. 60081, *Shotover*, crept alongside, the battle continuing as we raced side by side with both locomotives taken to their limits and both sets of men trying to outdo their opponents.What a thrilling sight it was to see her motion spinning as she also took a battering.

By this time most of the passengers in both trains had got in on the action with almost every window appearing to have a head stuck out jeering at each other, the noise from the combined six cylinders of the two locomotives was by now deafening as neither crew would yield in the race to York. All good things must come to an end and someone must lose in any contest. Our deciding factor proved to be a distant a couple of miles further on and Stan had to slam the regulator shut and drop the cut-off to 70% before fiercely applying the brakes. The following home signal was on as our speed ebbed away and the driver and fireman of *Shotover* gave us a victory wave as they pulled in front. With the vacuum gauge showing zero we stopped at the offending signal with just a wagon length to spare. "I didn't think we were going to stop" gasped Stan "But never mind it was a close fought thing."

Only a couple of minutes later the junction was clear, the home and starter signals came off and my mate eased open the regulator to take us out onto the East Coast Main Line. We passed under Holgate bridge at the South end of York Station just as A4 Pacific No. 60008 *Dwight D Eisenhower* was departing with an up express bound for Kings Cross, and what a majestic sight she was with her streamlined casing glistening in the sun. As we ran into York's magnificent station with the huge curved roof the trainspotters ran about shouting "It's a Jub," and as we came to a stand they flocked around the cab as if it was the only one in the Country. I climbed down and hooked off ready to take her light to York M.P.D. for servicing and a well earned rest.

Once on the shed we left *Dauntless* in the capable hands of the shed staff who took her to the ashpits ready for fire cleaning, followed by coaling, watering, shedding and a thorough check over by the fitters ready for her next turn of duty. With 45717 now secure, my mate and I made our way to the staff messroom for some lunch and a cup of tea.

The first part of our return trip was another first for me as we were booked to work a Newcastle-Kings Cross from York as far as Leeds where we were relieved before working the Leeds to Red Bank empty newspaper vans. Following our lunch at the shed we made our way to the station and awaited the arrival of our train. I was just in mid-sentence of asking Stan what class of locomotive we will have when he replied "You tell me because it's running in," my heart almost flipped a beat as I noticed the smoke deflectors, "I can't fire that Stan it's

Plate 32. 'Jubilee' Class No.45646, *Napier,* departs Leeds City about 1962 with a Trans-Pennine excursion.

Photo, Jim Carter.

either an AI or an A2 and I've never been on one in my life." "Don't worry I'll help you all I can," was the only answer I received. The locomotive was A2 No.60512 *Steady Aim* and what a monster she appeared to be in her polished green paint that glinted in the sun. Once aboard it took me a couple of minutes to find out where everything was situated on my side of the footplate but once accomplished I did feel a bit more at ease. The Gateshead fireman had left a good thick bed of fire in the box and for that I was grateful. One thing I did like about 60512

Plate 33. A1 Pacific No.60142 *Edward Fletcher* is seen entering Leeds City with the 8.45am Newcastle-Liverpool Lime Street in the early 1960's. The locomotive will be detached at the east end of the station and replaced by an ex L.M.S. engine which will work the train forward as the 11.29am. Leeds-Liverpool..

Photo, Jim Carter.

was the driver and fireman's seats, not a square wooden board on a flip-up hinge like ours but a proper bucket seat with a good backrest filled with what appeared to be horse hair (The only time we got that was on the Britannias).

Departing from the Up Main platform was also a new experience. As the platforrn was on a right hand bend it was impossible to receive the tip off the guard so on the signal was an "R" board for the driver, as you see today at most stations. In addition there was a bell that sounded level with the cab in case the sun was shining on the board.(Why oh why can't they take note of that on todays railways).

On departure we were routed slow line to take us back towards Church Fenton, and once clear of the junction I just put two rounds in the box and operated the exhaust injector. I didn't realise at first what free steaming engines these were due to the very soft exhaust beat but with my way of firing I could not keep her quiet and I was sat down most of the way to Leeds.

Arriving at Leeds we were relieved by a set of Leeds men and in my mind I did not want to get off this free steaming locomotive but it had to be. We made our way to the parcels depot to pick up our return working back to Manchester, Red Bank Carriage Sidings. Our load was twelve empty newspaper vans with a Black Five, No.45210 on the front end. this run was rather uneventful except that we were routed back via Halifax, Sowerby Bridge, Hebden Bridge and Rochdale to Manchester. Once inside at Red Bank Sidings and the locomotive detached we returned light to Newton Heath and left her under the coaling plant for the disposal men. All that was left now was to make our way to the drivers lobby and after Stan had made out a repair card we duly signed off duty. That was to be the last time I would be firing for Stan but not the last time we would be working together. Neither was it my last passenger firing turn on the Lanky as I volunteered to work my rest-day on the Saturday which was my very last day at Newton Heath, but this was to be a nightmare as I was paired with one of the most notorious drivers at the shed for the afternoon.

On that eventful Saturday afternoon I was rostered to work a Manchester to Barrow train as far as Preston with an old hand driver who shall have to remain nameless, but was noted for his heavy handed working of any locomotive that was assigned to him. He was the talk of the shed and most of the firemen would rather book off sick than work with him but as I had never had the privilege I could not criticise at that time. He, (the driver) was a short, wiry man in his sixties and looked rather comical with his greasetop cap that was pulled well down on his head and appeared to rest on top of his ears with the peak almost covering both eyes. Following booking on at 4.0pm.pm we received our locomotive off the foreman, the engine in question was one of Newton Heath's own Jubilees, No.45700 *Amethyst,* which was first out on number ten road and had already been prepared for us by the shed men so all that was needed was the fire spreading and the lamps placed on the middle centre brackets ready to go light to Queens Road Carriage Sidings. Once the handbrake had been released we dropped down to the shed outlet signal and I contacted the signalman at Thorps Bridge Junction signalbox to inform them that the engine for the Barrow was ready to come off shed. Once in the sidings I coupled the locomotive to the seven coach corridor stock and arranged the lamps on the two front bottom outside brackets to signify express passenger train. Up to that time not one word had passed between us so I climbed aboard and opened the steam heating cock to put about 40psi of steam through the train just as the ground signal came off for us to drop down into Victoria .

Plate 34. Stanier 'Jubilee' No.45698 *Mars* attracts the attention of schoolboy spotters at Manchester Victoria about 1962 as she slowly departs with a Liverpool Exchange-York morning service. On arrival at York the engine will be turned on York shed prior to working a return afternoon train.   Photo, Jim Carter.

Whilst stood in platform twelve with just four minutes to go I decided to build up the fire at the back of the box. Then he spoke for the first time. "What the hell is that?" he said, 'there's not enough coal in that box, fill it up," so I placed another two dozen rounds in the box but he was still not satisfied. "I want it full to the brick arch" he said. The logic in that I just could not see as I knew the engine would end up blowing it's brains off. With just thirty seconds to go the safety valves started to lift so I operated the live steam injector. "Right" he said, "leave that on and look out for the tip off he guard." "Right Away" I shouted across the cab and he opened the regulator and slammed the cylinder drain cocks shut.

Leaving Victoria was nothing spectacular as Stan would have put up a better performance and I began to wonder what was wrong with the other firemen at the shed. The going was still easy as we passed Deal Street box, on through Salford Station and round the long curve towards

Windsor Bridge Junction (Now named Salford Crescent). Once passed the junction I found out why he had a reputation as the cut-off was screwed down to no less than 60% and the regulator opened up to full. *Amethyst* sounded like a set of bongo drums as she threw out most of the live fire from the chimney end to cascade down and bounce on the roof of the coaches. It appeared to me that the fifth of November had arrived early as we tore up the bank passing Agecroft power station with fireworks flying in all directions and me wondering what to do next.

My driver soon rectified this last problem with a hefty shout over the roar of the locomotive. "Put two more rounds in the box and it will do to Bolton," he bellowed; this I did then slumped on my seat as we tore through Clifton Junction, Kearsley, Farnworth and Moses Gate stations.

The next point of interest was Bolton Shed which was situated on the left hand side of the railway just before Burnden Junction where the line to Bury took off to the right and appeared to go all the way around Bolton Wanderers football ground, (It must have been a fantastic place to watch the matches). On shed that Saturday was quite a mixture of motive power that ranged from Austerities, Crabs, Class 8s, Black 5's and various tank locomotives. All this I took in before he started braking for our stop at Bolton, Trinity Street.

As the platform was on the drivers side of the engine I did not need to look out for the tip off the guard but started to gas up the old girl again in readiness for our undoubted spirited departure once we cleared Bolton West Junction. My assumption soon became reality when the guard gave the right away, for, with a hefty upward pull on the regulator and the cut-off in full forward position *Amethyst* responded immediately and shot out a roar from the chimney end that would have scared a Lion out of it's skin. Once clear of the West Junction the reverser was screwed back a couple of turns and the regulator pushed to the horizontal position as the firework display started all over again as we headed towards Lostock Junction. On the approach to Lostock , I topped up the tender water supply from the troughs and we clattered over the points where the line to the left goes via Westhoughton and Hindley to Wigan and Southport.

Now the speed began to rise as we dashed through Blackrod and Adlington before the blower was put on and the regulator slammed shut for our next station stop at Chorley. Once the station duties were completed and I had once again tried to fill the firebox we set off in spirited style towards Euxton Junction going under Park Road Tunnel and Chorley's famous 'Flying Arches' but at least now the going became easier as it was all downhill, soon arriving at Euxton Junction where our line joined up with the West Coast Main Line from London to Scotland.

Having cleared the Junction at 20mph, 45700 was again opened up as we passed Euxton Coal Sdings (I do recollect doing some train spotting at that location during the school years). We were going at a good clip through Leyland Station where you could see a sign on a wall with the words "London 200miles - Glasgow 200miles" Next we passed the big Leyland Motors

Plate 35. An October 1965 shot of 'Jubilee' Class No.45600, *Bermuda*, a Newton Heath engine, seen passing through Salford Station with the 9am. Manchester Victoria-Glasgow, deputising for a failed diesel.

Photo, J.A.Oldfield.

works on the left and over Farington Junction where the line to Blackburn and Yorkshire left us to the Right. At that point my driver shut off steam for the last time to let us coast down the bank past Skew Bridge and started to brake the train on the approach to Ribble Sidings and we clattered over the River Ribble bridge ready for our final stop at Preston.

Following our relief by a set of Barrow men, we only had to make our way back to Newton Heath on the next return service travelling as passengers. "I understand that this is your very last day at Newton Heath" said my driver, "Yes" I replied, "I go back to Preston on Monday." "How far do you live from here?" was his next question. "Just outside Chorley," I answered. "Well if you have no reason to go back to the shed, get out at Chorley and I'll sign you off duty when I get back." I had no reason to go back as I managed to clear out my locker etc, earlier in the week ,so on arrival at Chorley I said my last goodbye as I detrained.

Although my time at Newton Heath was very short I found it a very enjoyable experience and will never forget my time at 26A, the biggest shed on the ex- Lancashire and Yorkshire Railway. But most of all I will remember the men like Andy Courtley, Bert Simmister, Billy Hill and last but not least, Stan Booth.

In 1995, as a driver for Intercity Cross-Country, I worked a train to Birmingham New Street and whilst having lunch a driver from Longsight Depot approached me and we could not believe our eyes as this driver was a fireman at Newton Heath at the same time as myself, namely Paul Winstanley and one of the first things he said to me was, "did you ever manage to fire for ***** ****?" What days they were, working with the BLEEDERS. (As Newton Heath men were known to all on the railway at that time.)

Plate 36. A filthy, unidentified Capprotti Class Five at Windsor Bridge, Salford, with the 16.10 Manchester Victoria-Southport in March 1961. These Stanier, taper boilered Class 5's were first introduced in 1934; the Capprotti versions however, appeared rather later on the scene, being introduced in 1948, some with Timken roller bearings and double chimney.

Photo, J.A.Oldfield.

Plate 37. Burnden Junction as it was. In preserved L.M.S. livery, 4-6-2 'Princess' Class No.6201 *Princess Elizabeth* makes a fine sight passing Burnden Junction's impressive signal gantry with a Princess Elizabeth Society Tour, 'The Red Rose' on 27th September 1980.   Photo, J.A.Oldfield.

Plate 38. Stanier Class 5, No.44978 is seen working a Manchester-Blackpool service at Blackrod in the early 1960's.

Photo, Alex Mann.

CHAPTER SIX
RETURN TO PRESTON

Following my return to Preston on 12th March 1962, Monday morning had me on duty at 10am for the station pilot with an old hand driver by the appropriate name of Harry Preston and this brought my total firing turns up to 322. Harry was a thick set man and it was obvious that in his younger days he had possessed an athletic body in order to fire the Claughtons, Prince of Wales, Experiments and Jumbos on the Premier Line. Our locomotive for the shift was a class 3F, 0-6-0T No.47472, that now belonged to nearby Lostock Hall M.P.D.,and was one of the shunting engines fitted with a screw wheel reverser that the drivers preferred to the pull over lever as fitted to most of the class. That first day was like a holiday after working the Blackpool and York expresses from Newton Heath and at 5.30pm. our relief climbed aboard to take her to the shed.

Tuesday morning saw me with a different driver named Jack Neil (Who left the railway some years later) and we were rostered to work the Ribble - Heysham fully fitted goods and return with the Heysham - Warrington mixed bag. After signing on duty at 8.00am. we picked up our locomotive in the old shed where it had been left earlier by a set of Crewe North men and it did look decidedly odd standing on it s own, in the dilapidated surroundings with two Patriots that were waiting to go for breaking up. Our locomotive was Jubilee No.45556 *Nova Scotia,* looking like she was not long out of the shops with the smell of new paint and the motion in a clean state. Once all was ready, I rang Preston No.5 signalbox to tell the signalman that the locomotive was ready to leave the old shed for the ten-o-clock Heyshams and no sooner had I climbed aboard than the ground signal came offwith a dull 'Clunk' as Jack released the vacuum brake and opened the regulator. With a great escape of steam from the cylinder drain cocks *Nova Scotia* made her first move out onto the goods line en-route to Ribble Sidings. Only a matter of minutes later we ran over the River Ribble bridge and into the yard where our train of 52 wagons lay strewn about the yard but after a couple of shunts lasting only five minutes we were all backed up and ready to depart.

A couple of minutes later our guard, Bob Scott arrived, and after the usual "Good morning men" he told us that we had now got 50 on as two of them were red carded and they would have to stay at Preston. Just give me time to get back and you can get this show on the road and with his large leather guards bag over his shoulder started the long walk back to his brake van.

Three or four minutes later Jack whistled up and with the signal off opened the regulator gently to take up the slack in the train couplings. Once out onto the goods line we received the tip from the guard as we passed Preston No.l box. With the distant signal showing off and a fullhead of steam, the regulator was opened up in earnest for the short, but steep gradient at the North end of the station. Running adjacent to the old No.1 platform (Which is now part of the parcels concentration depot) we got quite a few looks of amasement from the passengers awaiting the local service to Blackpool as we thundered through.

A matter of moments later we were clear of the station and running under the massive gantry with it s 16 signals and 9 subsidiarys at 30mph. Once clear of the gantry the line levelled out as we passed No.5 signalbox on our right, and behind the box stood a large building at the side of the Longridge branch "Durex Felt Works" standing out in bold letters. This used to be a small source of entertainment to the male passengers and an embarasment to the female of the species.

Over on our left we passed the old shed as we forked to the right under Pedder Street bridge to take us on our way to Lancaster (The left fork goes to Blackpool and Fleetwood).

Passing Oxheys Cattle Dock ,45556 was on full cry as I began to fire some more coal into the ever greedy box and a column of black smoke erupted from the chimney to be 'shot' skywards with the three cylinder beat. Since departing Ribble Sidings the live steam injector had been singing away and I only needed to use the exhaust injector to top the boiler up. Approaching Barton & Broughton I had a lean out of the window and felt the rush of cold air hitting my face before getting ready to pick up water from Brock Troughs.

Whilst leaning out it was always customary to clean the wind deflector glass, and no matter how dirty the locomotive appeared to be you never saw a dirty glass. "Right Bob, get ready with the scoop," my mate shouted above the rumble of the bouncing footplate. "If we fll up here it will do us," and with those words I went and stood behind Jack to unhook the safety chain from the water scoop handle in readiness to top up the 4000 gallon tender tank. "Now" yelled Jack as I started to turn the scoop handle in a clockwise direction to lower the scoop into the trough. With a rumble the water gauge started to rise 2500,3000,3500 and I started to ease the scoop out of the trough, just as the tender gauge was showing 4000 gallons.

After brushing the spilled coal from the footplate boards with my little hand brush I again took a breather and cleaned the wind deflector glass, looking back to make sure our guard was still following us in his brakevan and that none of the train axle boxes were running hot. By now we were passing through Garstang & Catterall Station at a speed of about 40mph with the cut-off wound back to 30% and the regulator just 'cracked' open. This speed was maintained until we were well past Bay Horse where Jack saw the distant for Oubeck was 'on'. So he put on the blower, shut the regulator and began to gather the train up with the brake so as not to wrap our guard around the brakevan stovepipe before applying the brake harder as we came nearer to the offending signal which was still stubbornly showing 'All on.' As we neared the signal however, it cleared allowing us to proceed into the Goods Loop. Once the brakevan was clear inside the loop and we had stopped at the signal, my mate climbed off the footplate in order to phone the signalman and I once again began to clean up with the handbrush and degging pipe. Within a couple of minutes 45556 was looking clean and fresh and Jack climbed aboard in readiness for our departure after the down Euston-Glasgow express had rushed past.

What a magnificent sight it was to see the express hurtle by, headed by 46238 *City of Carlisle* in maroon livery thundering on it's way north. After the express had cleared the section, the points went over and our signal cleared to take us on towards Lancaster. The short hop to Lancaster proved uneventful and speed increased as we descended Ripley Bank to take us through Lancaster Castle Station on the Through Road and over the River Lune. Morecambe South Junction's distant was 'on' and as we approached the home signal gantry, the left peg came off to take us off the West Coast Main Line and onto the Morecambe branch through Bare Lane Station and over the level crossing before arriving in the Goods Loop at Morecambe Promenade Station.

Plate 39. Heysham Moss Sidings at June 1965, as one of the Lancaster Green Ayre-Morecambe branch 25kv electric sets approaches, M28219 leading.   Photo, Alex Mann.

The shunter was waiting for us as we arrived in order to detach the locomotive allowing us to run around the train for our final leg to Heysham Moss Sidings. This we had to do tender first and it could be a nasty experience on a wet day, but on this day the weather was fine and once recoupled we set off down the branch. At Torrisholme a certain gentleman had a crafty way of saving on his fuel bills. He always put some bottles and tin cans on a home made shelf in his back garden and every train that passed sent a barrage of coal from the locomotives as both drivers and firemen tried to knock them off. As soon as every train had passed he would go out and pick up the coal for his own fire and replace any cans that had been knocked down. On arrival at our destination *Nova Scotia* was detached and coupled to our return working and as we were now engine first we did not go into Morecambe but went straight on at Torrisholme to run via Lancaster Green Ayre and rejoin the main line at Lancaster Castle (This line is now a public walkway, thanks to Dr Beeching). On arrival at Preston we were relieved by a set of Warrington men who took the train forward to Arpley sidings.

An incident occurred just two weeks later whilst working the same train to Heysham Moss with driver Tom Williams and 'Patriot' Class No.45543, *Home Guard*. All went well until Galgate, (South of Lancaster) where a platelayers cabin was sited on the left hand side. A platelayer was standing outside with his arms outstretched, indicating that he needed a cob of

Plate 40. The now vanished Lancaster Green Ayre Station, seen here in May 1949; a little before my time perhaps but a location I remember well from our trips to Heysham. In this view one of the ex Midland compounds, No.1005, is seen with a Morecambe train.

Photo, W.D.Cooper.

coal for the cabin stove. As luck would have it we had a very large piece on the footplate floor awaiting breaking up for the firebox, so the cab door was opened and the offending piece of best Yorkshire was placed ready to be slid off as we passed. Our speed at this time was in the region of 40mph and on a signal from Tom I gave a hefty push with my right boot and launched the cob into mid-air. On hitting the ground outside the cabin door (Which happened to be open) the projectile shot into the cabin, hit the top of the table and was last seen shooting out of the closed window at the other end, needless to say we did not hang about to see the outcome of this incident.

By this time the new English Electric type 4 diesels (Later class 40s) were coming on the railway scene to take over the West Coast express passenger services but steam locomotives were still in the majority covering at least 90% of the West Coast workings

Just two weeks later I was rostered as a fireman in the 'Sunshine' or local trip link and one of the more mundane jobs at Preston was taking the station pilot locomotives to nearby Lostock Hall shed for fire cleaning, watering and coaling, then returning them back to the station. For this working we had to sign on duty at the anti-social time of 7.50pm., but it did have one slight silver lining. This being that once the locomotive disposal was completed we could adjourn into the local hostelry for a well earned amount of liquid refreshment before returning to Preston with the engine, with it's cab usually packed full of men requesting a lift home and on most occasions complete with their push bikes which were positioned on top of the coal on tender engines or even on top of the side tanks of tank locomotives (How those cycles never fell off I will never know). Locomotives were shuttled backwards and forwards prior to being relieved and signing off duty at the ungodly hour of 3.50am.

On 26th March 1962, I was again rostered to do the night Lostock Hall runs with locomotives Nos.47362 and 42433, with an old hand driver who again shall have to remain nameless, but who lived in Wigan, approx 19 miles south of Preston. This driver always came to work in white bleached overalls and even after a full week of this dirty job his overalls were still as white and clean as on the first day. This was achieved by his uncanny ability to do absolutely nothing on arrival at the shed except make a bee-line into the local, leaving his fireman to do everything on his own.

The firemans compensation for this was for the driver to buy him a single gill on his arrival at the pub. (No wonder everyone called him Mother Goose)

Other work in this link included the 'Pilling Pig' morning and afternoon 15 targets that tripped between all the local yards along with the Deepdale and Courtaulds tripper and station pilot duties, so it was no wonder that it was called the sunshine link as apart from the Lostock Hall job all the other workings were in daytime.

A rather amusing incident occurred on 20th March 63, whilst working the local trip to Deepdale Coal Depot and the I.C.I "Red Scart" works sidings at Courtaulds, both located on the steeply graded Longridge branch. This job was now incorporated into the morning 15 target working and could be heavily loaded with household coal and wagons for Courtaulds.

My driver for the day was Sammy Waterworth, with Arthur Gilbert in the brakevan of the unfitted train, and Austerity 2-8-0 No. 90675 of Lostock Hall Shed at the business end.

The branch left the main line by the side of No.5 signalbox and immediately passed Maudland Yard on the left. Once on the Longridge branch you had to let yourself into Maudland Yard via a manually operated ground frame and once unlocked you could take out the single line token key for the branch and whilst you had this token in your possession no other train could use the branch until you returned back to Maudland Yard.

Plate 41. One of the Stanier 2-6-4T's used for local passenger services, No.42480 is seen on Lostock Hall Shed in 1963. These locomotives were the mainstay of the Preston to Southport and Preston to Wigan services.

Photo, Mick Howarth.

On the day in question we had a full load and ran onto the 1 in 54 gradient and into the 862yards long Deepdale Tunnel. The locomotive was down to a crawl in the tunnel and both the heat and smoke were almost unbearable as Sammy asked if the boiler was O.K. I replied that the boiler water level was just over three quarters full and the fire well built up with steam on full pressure.

By this time we were just over half way through the tunnel as he told me to get off the footplate and walk out of the tunnel and climb back aboard once the engine emerged into the daylight. This I did and I noticed that Sammy was walking behind me. There was nobody on the footplate!.

Sammy explained that all we had to do was wait for the locomotive and re-board. We could still hear the beat of the engine working very hard but strangely it appeared to be going away from us, saying this to Sammy he replied "Rubbish, it will come out any second" but it never did, as the weight of the train had caused the locomotive to slip to a stand pulling it back into Maudland Yard. Luckily the guard realising the train was out of control applied the handbrake in his van averting what could have been a major incident but got a real shock when he found no men on the footplate. Walking back to Maudland through the tunnel with no light was even worse than sticking it out on the engine and Sam got a severe reprimand for his actions but somehow managed to talk his way out of it.

Another amusing incident happened a couple of years later with driver Harry Ridding on the same working with austerity 90720. That day there was no traffic for Courtaulds and with only the Deepdale coal to haul was lightly loaded. All went well until we reached Deepdale Junction and after a few pops on the whistle, we noticed that there was still no movement from the signalbox. As the box also operated the level crossing gates for the main road we assumed that there must be a build up of road traffic and as we were running early the signalman had decided to clear the backlog before accepting us. Some five minutes later there was still no sign of us moving so to the box we went, only to find nobody at home, on his desk was a note saying he had gone to signal 43. This had to be some sort of code as his total signals only amounted to six. "Right" said Harry, you go back on the footplate and I'll open the gates to the railway and set the points, when you see the ground signal come off, bring the train up over the crossing and I'll put you into the coal yard. This I did has Harry stayed in the box. After shunting the loaded wagons in and the empties out, I took the train back over the crossing as Harry set the points back down the branch and came back to the footplate to take the train back to the North Union Yard at Preston. It was whilst awaiting relief that I mentioned to Harry what a brilliant idea I thought it was of his to operate the box ourselves. A look of horror came over his face and he replied, "My God, I've forgot to put the gates back."

I remained in the sunshine link until the end of June 1963, when I moved into the control link with a variety of drivers. In this link the jobs could be anything, as you were working to orders from Railway Control and you could end up anywhere on the system, from station pilot to places like Liverpool, Manchester, Huddersfield, Blackpool, Carlisle, Horwich Loco Works, Heysham, Warrington, Crewe or even London or Glasgow, provided tour driver had signed the road. The locomotives where also as varied from a class 0F 0-4-0, to a Coronation Pacific or English Electric type 4 diesel. The only fly in the ointment was the fact that I had a lot more night and early morning shifts to contend with compared with the 'Sunshine' link but at least I had my own mode of transport by this time in the shape of a 500cc Triumph/Norton motor-cycle to get me the 14 miles from home to Preston station.

One of my own favourite workings was the Huddersfield Royal Mail Travelling Post Office train. This train started from Workington in Cumbria, with a Workington train-crew as far as

Barrow-in-Furness, then Preston men to Preston to be relieved by another set of Preston men for the trip to Huddersfield and back. The train usually consisted of one letter sorting coach complete with post office personnel and three or four parcel vans with stops at Barrow, Ulverston, Grange-over Sands, Carnforth, Lancaster, Preston, Bolton, Manchester Victoria, Stalybridge and finally Huddersfleld. Motive power could be anything from a Stanier Black Five or Jubilee, to a class 24, 25 or 40 diesel provided they were fltted with a steam heating boiler in the winter months. The job I prefered most was the run from Preston to Huddersfield and back to Preston as time itself did seem to fly and you appeared to be back at Preston as soon as you had set off but the time on and off duty was certainly a minus having to sign on at the unrespectable time of 7.40pm., and not sign off until 3.40am. On arrival at Huddersfield with a steam locomotive, we were relieved by another set of men to take the engine away and await another one coming on at the other end of the train for our return working, but if a diesel was doing the working we ran it around the train and went for a bite to eat. The return working was very quick as we were only booked to stop at Manchester Victoria and Preston.

Even in later years as a driver, and single manned it was still one of my favourite jobs and I worked it right up to it's last year of operation in the late 1970s. I only ever heard of one amusing incident on that particular job all the time it ran and it concerned a driver by the name of Cyril Brayshaw or just "Brash" to the men, and a Black 5, 4-6-0 No.45025.

On leaving Preston he decided that he would top-up the tender water from Lostock Troughs near Bolton to save some time, but on passing it was noted that the troughs were dry so now he would have to put the bag in at Bolton once all station duties were completed, this entailed drawing the train up to the far end of the long platform where the water column was located. The only trouble was he did not tell anyone what he was about to do and on receiving 'Right Away' the train set off then came to a sudden stop. This train was monitored throughout it's journey by the civil police who were in constant touch with railway control following the great train robbery. Cyril's mate had just climbed onto the back of the tender and inserted the bag when the goods yard became full of police cars and vans with blue lights flashing and sirens blaring. Cyril who always stuttered when talking became even worse as he tried to explain to the officers what the hold-up was. The signalman at Bolton East Junction had informed control that the mail train had stopped out of course for no apparent reason and thinking the worst after the train robbery they in turn had requested police assistance who scared the living daylights out of poor Cyril.

On 16th December 1963, I was rostered to sign on duty at 3.40am to work a 'Special' Christmas parcels train to Carlisle with driver Cyril Bull who was a friendly sort of chap and who later became a footplate inspector at Preston. Following our signing on duty and reading the late notices we made our way down to the station to make a brew and await the arrival of our train, code number 3Z23, which was due to depart at 4.20am. At 4.15 we were told that the train was now running into platform 5 (This is now platform 3) so we made our way out of the cabin to mingle with the porters and post office workers who were present in abundance alongside a stack of Christmas mail bags. What a sight met my eyes as I looked up the platform to see a Coronation Pacific take the slight right hand bend into the station with what seemed like an endless train of parcels vans on tow. The locomotive in question was 46237 *City of Bristol* and a look at the smokebox shedplate of 12B told me it was a Carlisle, Upperby, locomotive. She looked splendid in her B.R. Standard Green livery shining under the station lights and it does seem a shame that only nine months later she would be withdrawn from service having covered almost 2 million revenue earning miles.

Relieving the set of Crewe men we were told she was a 'Good un' and we had twenty one mixed vans behind. The next person on the scene was our guard Paul Douthwhaite to give us the same information plus a special stop order for Penrith to now make us Lancaster, Penrith and Carlisle. At 4.22.,the signal came off and the right away was given just as the locomotive boiler pressure that was now showing 250psi on the pressure gauge, decided to lift the safety valves and a roar of steam shot into the night sky then abruptly stopped as Cyril released the brakes and gave an upward heave on the regulator to get the long and heavy train in motion for it's remaining ninety mile run to the border city. With a heavy muffled beat she started to move as the six foot nine inch driving wheels gripped the rails and never even tried to slip as we proceeded under Fishergate bridge and passed the long No.4 signalbox with all distant signals off.

Passing the old shed, the cut-off was screwed back a few turns and the regulator opened up in earnest as 46237 started doing what she was built for and the mufffled beat increased to a roar and the fire became pure white hot. Passing Oxheys she was well into her stride as the speedometer crept up from 30, to 40 and then 50mph, and I tried to keep the firebox topped up in the back corners while the exhaust steam injector sang away merrily to keep the boiler just over three quarters full of water. Throughout all this Cyril had never looked into the cab once but kept his head out of the window all the time to try and see the poorly lit semaphore signals as they loomed out of the inky black sky. As the speedometer needle touched 60mph he slammed the regulator shut then immediately just cracked it open again as the exhaust went back to a muffle.

Approaching Barton & Broughton Loop, I noticed a mixed goods train inside, hauled by a Stanier class eight 2-8-0 awaiting our passage and as we thundered past I could see a look of astonishment on the rather young firemans face and I remembered how I did the same on seeing a Coronation rush past sometime earlier in my career. Passing White Horse I noticed that the tender water was down to 2000 gallons so I positioned myself behind my mate and awaited his shout to drop the scoop and a few moments later we dashed over the troughs at Brock.

As the scoop went in, the tender water gauge started to rise, 2500, 3000 and 3500 as I started to lift it out and once clear the gauge was showing 4000 gallons with not a drop overflowing

(Unlike with the firing instructor.) On passing the creamery just north of Garstang & Catterall Station I took a look out of the left hand side of the cab to see my old stamping ground in the shape of the Pilling branch that veered off the W.C.M.L. sharply to the left on it's way to Garstang Town, and remembered what happy times I had with drivers like Arthur Duxbury, Jas Harrison and George Beardswood as we plodded through Nateby and Omo Crossing on our way to Pilling. (The line had only this year been cut back to Garstang Town and was to close completely in 1965). As we passed the goods loop at Oubeck, Cyril put on the blower, slammed the regulator shut and turned the reversing screw to full forward gear before starting to brake for our first stop at Lancaster Castle Station. On descending Ripley Bank it was always the fireman task to sight the signal as it was situated on a right hand curve and could not be seen by the driver due to the length of the boiler, but on a given signal from myself he knew he had a clear run into the platform.

On arrival at platform three, the porters and post office staff looked like a swarm of ants as a mixture of post bags and parcels were thrown in and out of the train and in just a few minutes with the signal at the end of the platform loop showing clear the whistles started blowing and green lights shining towards the locomotive as Cyril gave a pop on the Stanier whistle, Closed the cylinder drain cocks and once again gave an upward heave on the regulator handle to get the train in motion. As the train cleared the North end of the loop and and was nicely on the recently refurbished River Lune bridge the cut-off was screwed back a few turns and 46237 was opened up in earnest in order to get another dip in Hest Bank Troughs; she was really in her stride as we thundered over the points at Morecambe South Junction. Once the water top-up had been completed I returned to tending to the fire as we tore through Bolton-Le-Sands and Carnforth with the locomotive acting like a bucking bronco as it clattered over the points at the North and South Junctions in readiness for the assault on Yealand Bank.

The bank was no problem to the Stanier Pacific and once over the crest, *City of Bristol* again picked up speed as she raced down the other side towards Burton & Holme.

There is a public house on the right hand side at Burton & Holme with a semaphore home signal in the yard and during licensing hours the signal is pulled off to indicate to the local farmers that the bar is open and after last orders it is put back to the danger position. This local landmark can still be seen to this day.

Once passed Burton & Holme No.2 signalbox with it's long Down Goods Loop, the locomotive is going at a good clip as we rush towards the very small station at Milnthorpe and once through, 46237 has to start working hard as it is all uphill through Hincaster Junction, Oxenholme and onto Grayrigg bank. Peat Lane and Hay Fell were passed as the speed started to ebb away with the Coronation' sounding like a set of bongo drums as Cyril tried to keep the rate as high as possible. As we passed the very small ex L.N.W.R. signalbox at Lambrigg Crossing she appeared to be holding her own and by the time we crested the summit at Grayrigg the speed was still a respectable 50mph. Speed increased as we passed Low Gill and headed down into the Lune Gorge, where, on the right a clump of trees were formed into the shape of a heart to represent the 'Heart of Cumbria'.

Cyril had given no whistle code to the signalman at Grayrigg box to request the assistance of a banker at Tebay for the climb to shap summit so he must have thought *City of Bristol* was more than capable of taking it in her stride, for although the train was long the vans were not as heavy as coaches. By now we were travelling between 75 and 80mph and I started building up the fire in readiness for the 1 in 75 uphill climb to Shap summit and once this task was completed, I yet again stood behind my mate in order to get our final water top-up from Dillicar Troughs at Tebay.

As we raced through Tebay the injector was singing away so I closed the firehole doors and a column of black smoke erupted out of the chimney end into the crisp thin air. On passing the tiny level crossing box at Scout Green the speed was decreasing rapidly as Cyril screwed the cut-off down another turn and 46237 responded by trying to awaken every Curlew in the area while I continued to feed the ever hungry firebox and hoping that I would soon see the Bridge of Sighs just north of Shap Wells. Scout Green box once had a model of a spitfire fighter plane on a pedestal just outside the box door following W.W.II., and I have often wondered where it went to as it did seem to vanish overnight.

Heading up the 1 in 75 gradient with a thick bed of coal in the firebox I noticed that the coal in the tender was getting rather far back so I decided to try out the coal pusher that was fitted

Plate 42. Ex-Eastern Region 'Britannia' No.70024 *Vulcan* is seen on the Down Fast near Leyland station on 24th July 1964.   Photo, W.D.Cooper.

Plate 43. Stanier Class 5 No.45126, complete with ballast plough, takes a dip from Dillicar troughs with a Crewe-Carlisle parcels train in the spring of 1963. Note the figure on the extreme left, none other than W.D.Cooper. He and Jim Carter were often to be seen together on photographic essays. Sadly, Mr Cooper passed away in December 1998 aged 93.

Photo, Jim Carter.

on the tenders of these fine locomotives. After opening the steam valve to activate the pusher, one pull and push on the long handle that was fitted on the tender shelf was enough to do the trick, as following a loud bang from the back of the tender a large amount of coal came crashing against the tender doors (That device saved a lot of scratting with the coal pick).

By this time the speed had been reduced to 30-35mph as we passed Shap Wells with the well known Shap Wells Hotel on our left with the statue of Queen Victoria in the grounds looking South as she still does to this day.

Finally, at long last I could see the Bridge of Sighs over the cutting just before the summit and no wonder it was also known as the firemans friend. We surmounted the summit at 30mph and at long last the hard work was over and *City of Bristol* had once again proved her worth.

Speed increased rapidly as we decended the other side passing Shap Quarry (Since renamed Hardendale) and the now closed Shap Station that still boasted it's short platforms and station buildings. Harrisons Sidings with its Down Loop, Thrimby Grange with it's Up Loop, Bessie Ghyll curve and Eden Valley Loop were all passed, and at long last we ran into Penrith Station with it's Down Passenger Loop where a mixed freight, hauled by an Austerity 2-8-0 was awaiting our departure.

Station duties only lasted a few moments to remove a dozen bags and a brand new 'Raleigh' push-bike for some lucky youngster who was certainly going to have a merry Christmas and in no time at all the doors were slammed shut and the right away was given and Cyril got us on the move again for the last leg of the journey to the Border City.

Kitchen Hill was passed with the locomotive still accelerating on the down grade towards Plumpton as an up sleeping car train passed us with another 'Coronation' at it s head with about fourteen in tow. Plumpton Station was closed by now but still retained the Up Loop and signalbox. When the station was open it boasted a large bell that was operated by the signalman when a stopping train was approaching to indicate to the station master who would be at home in his nearby cottage (What a life!). Once passed Plumpton the line is a mass of curves but I am busying myself running the fire down as the locomotive will be taken off at Carlisle and there is nothing worse for the disposers than a locomotive arriving on the ash pit with a full box of fire. As we pass Southwaite my task is almost at an end and I have time to sit down on the firemans seat and breathe in the beautiful fresh air while my mate is preparing to brake the long train after passing Wreay curve.

Plate 44. Stanier 8F No.48733 puts in some effort climbing Shap unassisted with a freight on 27th August 1959.
Photo, W.D.Cooper.

On the long straight section approaching Upperby South Junction the blower is put on and theregulator slammed shut for the last time as a hissing noise is heard as air is rushing into the vacuum brake valve and the train starts to slow, and on passing Upperby Shed I notice a mixture of different locomotive classes lined up on the ash pit road awaiting disposal and only moments later we are running into platform No. 1 to be relieved by a set of Upperby men who are taking her to the shed for a well earned rest and replenishment of coal and water before her next turn of duty.

Once relieved we make our way to the station mess room for a bite to eat and a welcome cup of tea as we await the morning passenger train back to Preston to sign off duty and make our way home.

I was feeling rather proud of myself following the run to Carlisle with *City of Bristol,* but little did I know what was in store for me six weeks later when I was notified that I was going into the 'Top Link' with driver Harold Critchley with workings that included the 2.40am. to Glasgow Central., and back with the 11.40pm. Liverpool and Manchester. The 10.40pm to London Euston., and back with the Ulster Express, and in the summer months the Windermere-London 'Lakes Express' which we were booked to work from Preston to Euston.

Plate 45. One of Sir William Stanier's 'Jubilee' Class locomotives No.45562 *Alberta* is seen at Carlisle in September 1967. Note the cabside stripe, denoting that the locomotive is banned from working south of Crewe beneath the wires.

Photo, D.Hill.

CHAPTER SEVEN
THE FINAL STEAM YEARS

Harold Critchley was a short, thick set senior driver in the top link at Preston and was easily recognisable without his hat by his completely bald head. In fact he had not got a hair on his body anywhere due to a medical condition that made it all fall out overnight; he went to bed one night and the following morning his bed was covered in hair! I was rostered with Harold as my first driver on transfer to the top link and despite his odd appearance he was a real gentleman.

The London and Glasgow workings were booking off turns which entailed staying in the railway barracks at either Camden in London, or Polmadie in Glasgow. The one at Camden was situated just across the road from Primrose Hill Station with the front rooms overlooking the main lines and Camden locomotive shed. The building still survives to this day but has now been transformed into private office units. Polmadie Barracks was sited on the west of the line running into Glasgow between Polmadie and Eglington Street Station overlooking the main line and the goods yards. This building has also survived to this day but is now in use as a home for wayward women. Both these barracks catered for the needs of the men including beds, dining hall, washrooms and recreational room equipped with snooker tables, dartboards etc., and it was always the policy to try and acquire a back bedroom if possible in order to cut down on the noise emanating from the railway to aid better sleep. Polmadie had the cleanest beds but Camden served the best food so it was a toss-up which was the best of the two.

By this time most of the West Coast Main, Line expresses were diesel hauled by English Electric type 4 locomotives and that included our own London and Glasgow workings ,but if no diesels were available or a failure ensued, then the jobs were entrusted to the tried and well tested 4-6-0 and 4-6-2 steam locomotives. The engine for our working to Glasgow was supplied by Edge Hill Shed in Liverpool. The return working was rostered to the locomotive that had arrived earlier in the evening with the 'Mid-Day Scot.' The London workings were entrusted to locomotives from Crewe North Shed. By this time both these sheds were allocated a stud of the new 2000hp diesels to be utilised on mainly express passenger workings and nine times out of ten it was one of these engines that we ended up with but sometimes fate can change all that as I found out on more than one occasion.

When these new diesels with their massive 10" bore and 12" stroke sixteen cylinder engines first came on the scene, they were greeted with a kind of love hate relationship by the men who had to work on them. In their favour was the fact that they were more than capable of working any train to steam engine timings with a lot less manual work from the footplate crews in a cleaner environment, but against them was their failure rate. Almost every day you could guarantee that one or more would fail on the main line. In the winter months the cab heating was totally inadequate consisting of one tiny fan heater situated on the floor under the master controller. This minuscule heater was incapable of keeping a can of tea warm let alone the cab.

Most of the engine failures were due to earthing problems, these locomotives had an earthing link fitted to them in the engine room control cubicle. This was thought to be the main cause of the problems by a lot of drivers and when preparing to take one off shed this was unbolted and thrown away. This unofficial crude and drastic measure did however appear to work as the failure rate on these locomotives almost fell to zero. This was a risky solution to the problem as should a earth fault occur with no weak link the results could prove catastrophic. They were all later fitted with a modified earthing system and electric cab heaters on the engine room bulkhead at foot level to improve their reliability and comfort respectively. From then on the men liked and trusted the Type 4's and got sterling work out of them until the arrival of the more modern and powerful 2750hp Brush Sulzer type 4, later class 47 locomotives.

As well as the London and Glasgow work, the top link had rostered work to Crewe, Carlisle, Windermere and Blackpool, with both diesel and steam power and on some of these jobs fine performances were achieved with the run down and unkempt steam locomotives.

One really outstanding performance was achieved on Tuesday, June 19th 1964, by Harold and myself with Britannia pacific No.70023, *Venus,* on the 1.10p.m. express as far as Crewe. (12.35 Blackpool North - Euston).This locomotive was in my opinion one of the best steaming

Plate 46. 'Britannia' No. 70023 *Venus*, backing onto a parcels train at Preston on 20th April 1966. She would depart from platform 2 for Crewe at 13.50 approx.   Photo, Mick Howarth.

Plate 47. 'Coronation' Class Pacific No.46239 *City of Chester* is seen with an Up express passing Leyland on 24th July 1964. By September of that year all these fine locomotives would have been withdrawn. Note the coal pusher in operation. Photo, W.D.Cooper.

engines of the class although it appeared in a very grubby state externally. Once clear of Preston South Junction, with the pull out regulator handle level with Harold's ear and the cutoff at 50%, I could tell she had lost none of her sparkle as the steam pressure gauge appeared to be stuck in the 240psi area and heavy firing was not needed with the ten coach train. This train was booked to stop at Wigan North Western and Warrington Bank Quay on it's fifty mile journey to Crewe.

All was going well as we ran into Wigan, spot on time, but on departure things were about to change. This happened when Harold saw the distant signal for Golborne Junction was showing on. As we approached the home signal gantry at a crawl the left hand one cleared to take us via Lowton Junction, Newton-le-Willows and Earlestown to rejoin the main line at Winwick Junction. As we ran over the bridge carrying us over the West Coast Main Line we could see what the trouble was in the shape of an engineers train in the cutting with a length of rail removed from the main line. This slow diversion had made us at least seven minutes late and as we ran into Warrington Bank Quay Station, a platform inspector confirmed that it indeed it was a broken rail causing the disruption.

On departure from Warrington, as we climbed the bank up to the Manchester Ship Canal bridge, my mate asked if the locomotive was alright from my point of view, to which I replied "she is one of the best of the class and you can do what you like with her." 'Right! well get her hot and we will see how well she can perform to Crewe, as there are some locomen in the first coach and I want to give them a run for their money." Those last words were like a shot in the arm to me as I fired six shovelfulls of coal into each back corner plus two full rounds into the rest of the box then slammed the doors shut and a column of black smoke shot skywards from the chimney end. Once over the canal bridge the speed increased rapidly on the down grade as Harold worked the cut-off to it's best effect and as we rushed over the small Norton Crossing the speedometer needle was well into the sixties.

Speed was still increasing as we darted into, and out of, Preston Brook Tunnel as we passed Weaver Junction signalbox where the line from Liverpool joins the W.C.M.L. Both signalmen had there heads out of the window to see the 'Riddles' Pacific in full cry. Acton Bridge and Hartford Stations were passed at an alarming rate,the passengers awaiting the Crew local all

Plate 48.Climbing steadily along the Up Slow Line at Balshaw Lane, Bidston based Standard Class 4, 4-6-0 No.75057, heads south with a train of empties in the early 1960's. Photo,Paul Tuson.

decided to stand well back from the platform edge and at Winsford Junction, Harold called me over to see the speedometer needle that was jammed on the 100mph stop pin. Crewe was reached two minutes early and as I went in between the tender and first coach to hook off I overheard a Crewe driver tell Harold that they had been having bets on what speed we would attain and he was astounded when told the needle was stuck on the magic 'Ton'.

Late 1964 and 1965 saw the express passenger steam locomotive classes dwindling at an alarming rate as the big diesels took a strangle hold of the top workings on the West Coast Main Line.

On the l9th of September 1964, I departed from home at the ungodly hour of 1.40am on my trusty motorcycle for the fourteen mile journey to Preston signing on point. On arrival, I signed on duty at 2.05am. in order to work the 2.40am. to Glasgow (Central) and back with the 11.40pm. to Preston. My driver on this occasion was Harry Mounsey who was later to become a very good friend of mine and after his retirement actually moved from Preston to live in the same village as myself. He was a tall athletic looking man but his main attribute was his handling of a steam locomotive as he could almost make them talk. Following our signing on and reading of the late notices to inform us of any late engineering works, no water in troughs etc., we made our way to the station to await the train which consisted of a portions from Liverpool and Manchester that had been joined up at Wigan. The Edge Hill locomotive would work it through to Glasgow.

At 2.33 the train ran into platform five with an English Electric Type 4 (Later Class 40) at it's head and what appeared to be a never ending line of sleeping cars and mark one coaches in tow. On relieving the Liverpool driver, we were informed that our loading was fifteen, and that the locomotive was a 'good un'; the engine in question was No.D318, (40 118) fitted with a Clayton steam generator and the racket from the 2000hp sixteen cylinder diesel engine was

Plate 49. Stanier class 5 No.45423 passes Taylors Lane, Wigan, with a southbound freight on 16th October 1962.
Photo, W.D.Cooper.

Plate 50. 'Coronation' Pacific No.46248 *City of Leeds* bowls along at Golborne Summit on the Up Fast line in mid 1962. The photograph is taken from the footbridge that once spanned the tracks here prior to electrification.

Photo, J.R.Carter.

deafening. Qnce aboard with the inevitable can of coffee, Harry did his obligatory move on these engines by removing his boots and replacing them with bedroom slippers for the 198 mile run.

At 2.40am., with all signals at green we received the tip from the guard and Harry got the locomotive on the move. With stops at Penrith, Carlisle, Lockerbie, Carstairs and Motherwell, and due in Glasgow at 7.20am.. The run to Glasgow was uneventful and the old girl never faltered once into her task and on arrival in platform No.l at Central Station we were relieved by a set of Polmadie men who would later take her away for refuelling and watering in readiness for her next trip South. Following our relief at Central station we made our way via the City streets to the lodging barracks at Polmadie for a wash, some breakfast and then to bed in our own single rooms. At 6pm their was a loud knocking on half a dozen doors as the knocker-up tried his best to rouse the Crew and Preston footplate men and guards, and by 6.30pm. we were up, washed and having some dinner in the dining hall, followed by a quick game of snooker in the games room.

At 7.45 Harry said that he didn't want to go to the staff club as was normal on these workings but wished to go to the local cinema to see the latest film., I agreed, and away we went. As we emerged from the cinema my mate said, "it's rather cold tonight, I hope those cab heaters are working better than normal". On arrival at Polmadie shed, Harry asked me to get the engine number and which road it was located on from the engine board while he visited the toilet. On arriving at the large board it read, "11.40 Liverpool, No.8 road, Loco No 46128". My heart sank as I could not believe it. I was still in a state of shock when Harry arrived on the scene and on seeing what I had seen said, "that can't be right as our locomotive is the one off the 'Mid-Day Scot', so into the foreman's office he dives to fnd out who the comedian was. The foreman explained that the board was correct as the Down Mid-Day Scot locomotive failed at Carlisle and was replaced by 46128, so that was our locomotive back to Liverpool. The Foreman said he was sorry, and that if he had got a spare main line diesel we could have had it, but he had three sets of men preparing the 'Scot'.

So off we went, rather dejectedly, to collect our engine where the scene resembled a swarm of ants around a jam pot, two drivers were oiling the outside motion, a fireman oiling the inside, another trimming the lamps but the one that got me was a fireman in the cab who was doing nothing but shovelling coal into the 31.25sq ft. of firebox, until I don t think he could have got another teaspoonful through the firehole doors. The fire was absolutely black and was totally against everything we had been taught. Once all the men were clear, the locomotive was again taken to the coaling stage to have her tender topped right up as that one fireman alone must

Plate 51. The scene at Beattock South on 18th June 1966, with one of the B.R. Standard 2-6-4 tank engines No.80111 in view.

Photo, J.A.Oldfield.

have put at least a ton in the box. Following the top-up, we took over the locomotive from the Polmadie men who said they could do no more with a "Have a nice trip Jimmy". The steam pressure was well down as as we went to the ringing out post but there was not a thing I could do about it so onto the phone I go to ring the signalman that the 11.40 Liverpool was ready for off shed, "Could I have the locomotive number please" he asked. When I told him the number all he said was "God help you" and the signal was cleared to take us off shed, through Eglington Street Station and into Glasgow Central.

Arriving at the long platform twelve, our train was waiting and after coupling up and putting some steam through for the train heating I went to make a can of coffee for the first part of our return trip, noticing that the fire was at last managing to claw it's way through all the coal in the box. While I was away Harry operated the injector to top-up the boiler as the steam pressure was now looking a bit more healthy, I had just returned to the locomotive when our

Plate 52. One of the McIntosh 3F, 0-6-0's No.57619 simmers on Polmadie Shed, Glasgow. Whilst I never worked on these locomotives I often came into contact with them here after working in from Preston.

Photo, Mick Howarth.

Plate 53. A view familier to generations of railwaymen would have been this outlook from the rear of Polmadie Barracks taken on one of my trips to Glasgow.

Photo, Author.

guard arrived on the scene to give my mate the loading of sixteen bogies and he too almost had an heart attack on seeing 46128, *The Lovat Scouts* on the business end, and wondering if he would manage to get home the following morning. We had just settled for a brew in the cab when we heard the sound of an English Electric engine coming ever closer and on looking out saw a small type 2, (later class 20) with it's long nose facing south and backing on to us cab first, and once the second man had tied on, the the driver told us they had orders to assist us as far as Carstairs. As the foreman felt he had let us down, the driver had requested to help us to Carlisle but the diesel was needed back at Glasgow for other duties. "You just keep the passengers warm and a breath of steam at the cylinders

and I'll rip the guts out of this thing," said the Scottish driver before returning to his cab.

At 11.40, with all the colour light signals at green the train was eased out of the long station platform, over Jamaica bridge and through the massive junction on the start of the long trek south. Once clear of Eglington Street Tunnel the little diesel gave an almighty roar as Harry opened up the 'Scot' to get some speed into the train and what a sight it was to see and hear both old and new locomotives working in unison. As we thundered past Polmadie Shed, both the Foreman and the men who had prepared *The Lovat Scouts* for this mammoth undertaking were stood at the side of the line to give us a wave and watch this awesome sight.

By Cambuslang a good speed had been attained, so Harry eased up our locomotive but the Polmadie driver left his flat-out all the way until approaching Motherwell for our first stop. As we ran into the station even the staff and some of the passengers looked surprised at this unique combination of motive power at the head of this heavy ovemight express. On departure both locomotives were opened up to try and get some speed on the uphill climb past Shieldmuir Junction, Wishaw (Central), Carriongill Junction and Law Junction (where the diversion line from Uddingston Junction via Bellshill and Holytown rejoins the mainline). Up to this point I had never touched the fire but just worked the injectors to keep the boiler topped up but I decided to give her a few rounds to keep a nice thick bed as I knew that once we had passed through Carluke Station we would be on another stiff climb until we got to the summit at Craigenhill. At Braidwood I looked out of the window to hear both locomotives working hard and the diesel was being worked so hard she actually had flames emitting from the exhaust, being thrashed on the bank. Once at the top of the climb, Harry shut off steam and left the rest of the pulling to the already red hot freight engine all the way past Lanark Junction until the brakes were applied for our next stop at Carstairs.

On arrival at Carstairs, I was rather sorry to see the Polmadie second man hook off from our locomotive, as I knew we were now going to lose our helping hand that had worked so hard for the last twenty-nine miles to leave us entirely on our own for the almost non-ending climb to Beattock Summit some twenty four miles away. Once the diesel had been detached and was on her way back to Glasgow, I replaced our lamps on the front of the locomotive to denote express passenger train and returned to the cab where Harry was shovelling coal into the box like someone demented until it was back level with the lip-plate. Some two minutes later I heard the whistles blowing and on looking back saw both the porters and guards lamps emitting a bright green light towards us. "Right away Harry", I shouted to my mate and he opened the regulator to full first valve and slammed the cylinder drains shut. At first nothing appeared to happen as she tried to move this heavy tonnage from a standing start but a matter of seconds later the massive 6ft 9in driving wheels started to move as her 33,150lb tractive effort took hold. Once clear of Carstairs Junction where the line to Edinburgh (Waverley) diverges off to the left we ran straight over the water troughs as I tried my best to top-up the depleted water supply and I had just about managed to get a full tank before we ran onto the bank as Harry screwed back the reverser two turns and opened the regulator to full second valve. I raised the scoop and slammed the firehole doors shut and put on the live steam injector to try and maintain the boiler water level. (This injector was left on all the time until we crested the summit) On the bank the old girl was struggling but the very short downhill grade to Thankerton helped a little in her quest for more speed but this was short lived as she hit the stiff climb up to Symington. After this point we have four miles slight down hill running to Lamington where the railway crosses over the river Clyde and Harry used all his skill to make the best use of the cut-off as I start to struggle with the fire again in order to try and keep the steam pressure needle as close to the 250psi red line as possible. By this time I was sweating so much that my body felt like I had jumped into the river we were about to cross. Once over the river bridge we hit the last part of the bank but this was only the beginning as it was all uphill for the next thirteen miles which would take us past Abington (with it's passing loops), the Village of Crawford, Bodsbury Level Crossing and finally over the summit with it's passing loops which we passed at 45mph.

Once over the crest of the summit the acceleration rose at a rapid rate on the steep downhill grade for the next ten miles to the foot of Beattock Bank to take us over Harthope Viaduct, (with the main A74 trunk road running underneath), Greskine and on past Auchencastle where the speedometer needle was stuck on the 100mph pin. Harry had now shut-off steam and just cracked open the regulator to keep the cylinder lubricators working. On looking out of the cab side the motion was a complete blur and I also noticed that the cab itself was shaking away from the side of the firebox so badly was she in need of a works visit.

Plate 54. Ex L&Y 'Crab' No.42720 seen near Greskine on Beattock Bank in the 1950's. An early morning shot with atmospheric results as the hot exhaust condenses in the cold air.

Photo, W.D. Cooper.

From Beattock Station the grade of the bank is reduced considerably but it is still downhill for the next five miles before levelling off to Lockerbie to take us through Murthat, Wamphray (where it starts to level off), Dinwoodie and over the level crossing at Nethercleugh. At Wamphray I refilled the back corners and under the doors, level with the lip-plate again and put four rounds around the rest of the box then closed the doors, put on the exhaust steam injector to top up the boiler and sat down to watch the countryside rush by until our booked stop at Lockerbie Station was reached. Harry on the other hand had still got his head out of the window trying to sight the poorly lit distant signals before operating the blower, opening the firehole doors, shutting the long regulator handle and start braking the long and heavy train from ninety miles per hour to a dead stop in the station platform to within a matter of feet.

During station duties I was busying myself trying to refill the ever hungry firebox and by the time the whistles started blowing for our departure I had managed to get a nice thick bed of fresh coal in the box and once again the back corners were full, and under the door it was level with the lip-plate. Once clear of the station she was opened out again and the exhaust beat from the three cylinders sounded even better to me than a top orchestra could produce. The going was still level at this point and 46128 started to accelerate at a slow rate but that was soon halted as we ran over the viaduct at Castlemilk, for now it was slightly uphill again for another two and a half miles. Once over the top of this short bank she recommenced her acceleration to take us through the Villages of Ecclefechan and Kirtlebridge, over Cove Level Crossing and through Kirkpatrick with still another thirteen miles to go to the Border City, but now the speed was building up well as I again gave the firebox four more rounds of coal before closing the doors and operating the injector. Harry was still fully occupied with his head out of the window, signal sighting as we tore through the well known railway disaster area of Quintinshill with it's up and down passing loops. What a sight it was to me another one and a quarter miles further on as I saw a large board by the side of the track with just one word , "England," standing out boldly as we went over the Scotland-England border at Gretna Junction and started on another downhill grade towards Floriston. I placed myself behind Harry to refill the depleted tender water from the water troughs, as soon as the tender was full I raised the scoop and secured it with the holding chain as we ran over the bridge spanning the Solway Firth, followed by Floriston Level Crossing. By this time I was feeling and looking more like a living corpse but just another couple of miles later Harry put on the blower, opened the firehole doors and closed the regulator as we passed the huge yards and engine shed at Kingmore, (12A) Carlisle. Harry was braking the train hard as we ran over the River Caldew, then Carlisle North Junction at 20mph before arriving at platform No.4 in the station after covering a total of 103miles with still around another 90 to go.

Arriving at the stop signal at the end of the platform, I opened the large tender doors in order to bring forward some of the remaining coal supply with the coal pick onto the shovelling plate while Harry grabbed hold of my brew can and flew off the footplate into the porters room to make us another brew of coffee.(Tea wasn't really any use on a steam locomotive as it only tended to stew then tasted horrid) In a matter of moments later he was back with a full can while I was still digging in with the pick, so he placed the can on the warming plate just over the firehole doors and took hold of the shovel then started refilling the firebox with a very thick bed of coal.

He had just finished with the fire when the whistles were blowing and green lights showing to tell him we were 'Right Away'. The signal at the end of the platform was also green with the letters "UF" to denote the route was set for the Up Fast Line. Following a pop on the whistle the regulator was opened to full first valve and the cylinder drains slammed shut as *The Lovat Scouts* started to move, but after just two turns of the driving wheels she decided to slip on the greasy rails and with an almighty roar shot a column of smoke and steam high into the night air as she fought for adhesion and Harry slammed the regulator shut until she found her feet then restarted the whole process again.

Once past Upperby shed ,(12B) I knew it was going to be a hard toil for both the locomotive and her crew as it was virtually all uphill to Shap Summit and there would be no rest at all until our next stop at Penrith. On passing Upperby South Junction we ran straight onto the

Plate 55. Ex Western Region 'Britannia' No.70028 *Royal Star,* is seen southbound near Dillicar with a fast through freight in the early 1960's.
Photo, Jim Carter.

notorious bank that would take us past Wrea, Plumpton Junction, Kitchen Hill and into Penrith Station (The southbound climb to Shap Summit was not as steep as the northbound but was considerably longer making it more demanding on the footplate crews). At Penrith, I once again dove into the tender to bring down some more coal before tending to the fire and boiler water supply then sat down with a brew and awaited our departure. By this time I was feeling both mentally and physically weak and my clothing was stuck to my skin with sweat.

As we departed and headed towards Eden Valley with it's curve and up passing loop Harry came over to my side of the footplate and told me to go to the other side and keep my eyes open but not to let our speed drop and he would fire her to the top of the bank.

I found that operating the locomotive from Harry's side of the cab was also no easy task as the semaphore signals were very poorly lit in the dark and trying to spot them was a job on it's own but coupled with the task of trying to keep up the speed of the heavy train on the stiff bank made it even worse. The rest from the shovelling came as a big relief on my sweating and eased my aching back as I stood leaning on the window ledge letting the night air cool me down as *The Lovat Scouts* continued thundering away up the bank through Bessie Ghyll curve, past Thrimby Grange, Harrisons Sidings and Shap Station. On looking over to the other side of the footplate all I saw was Harry sat on the firemans seat with his feet up on the toolbox cupboard with a cup of coffee in his hand but the boiler pressure was almost on the red line and the water level three quarters full. Once passed Shap Quarry (Now Hardendale) and approaching the summit at 916 feet above sea level my mate came back to take control of 46128 on the 1 in 75 downhill grade and I had at least regained some composure.

The descent of Shap bank was as alarming as the drop down Beattock with the locomotive gaining speed past Shap Wells where Harry once again closed the regulator and just cracked it open. I on the other hand had opened the firehole doors and operated the exhaust steam injector to top-up the boiler and also stop her from blowing off. By Scout Green the speed was well into the nineties as Harry made her do what she was built to do following her rebuild way back in June 1946, as she went down the bank like her original name of 'Meteor' suggested. After passing Tebay Station I again placed myself behind my mate for his signal to drop the water scoop into Dillicar Troughs and bring the tender capacity back up to 4000gals, and once achieved the scoop was raised and re-fastened with the holding chain. Once again I attended to the fire in order to keep it's bed thick at the back of the box for the slight rise up the Lune Gorge and past Low Gill to Grayrigg Summit. As we crested the summit with the injector singing away I could once again relax while Harry kept the train under control on the numerous curves that took us over Lambrigg Crossing, past Hay Fell and Peat Lane before darting through Oxenholme Station at 85mph and rattling over the points for the goods loop where an 8F hauled fully fitted freight awaited our passage before proceeding on it's way to Carnforth. Hincaster Junction and Milnthorpe were passed before I started with the firing again with four rounds all over the grate area and re-filling the back corners as we thundered past

Plate 56. Class 5 No.45439 blows off steam at Lancaster whilst waiting for the right -away. Note the A.W.S cylinder near the cab, fitted to most mainline steam locomotives in the 1960's.　　　　Photo, B.Nichols.

Burton & Holme and onto the short but stiff bank to the top of Yealand. Now it was all downhill again to our next stop at Carnforth where I operated the injector before once again delving into the tender with the coal pick to bring down some more coal onto the firing plate while Harry awaited the tip off the guard.

The 'Right Away' was given a few moments later and 46128 was opened up in earnest as my mate wanted to gain as much speed as possible by the time we reached the water troughs at Hest Bank. As we passed Bolton-Le-Sands Station and Level Crossing our speed was around fifty miles per hour, so I positioned myself behind Harry and awaited his signal to lower the scoop; once it had been given I kept my eyes on the water gauge and watched the pointer rising, 2000, 2500, 3000, 3500, I started removing the scoop as 4000gals filled the tank and we ran over Hest Bank Crossing and through the station. My mate shut off steam again before braking at Morecambe South Junction for our next to last stop at Lancaster, where I again started digging with the pick while Harry filled the firebox. Leaving Lancaster Castle Station southbound was no easy task with an heavy train as you were already on the I in 98 of Ripley Bank and next to no acceleration could be made on this short but stiff grade and even an express that did not stop had the wind knocked out of it. As we crested the summit the going got easier and the speed increased as we passed Oubeck with it's Up and Down loops that held a parcels train in each, as on the Down line another 'Jubilee' hauled express rushed past on it's way North.

Galgate, Bay Horse and Garstang were also soon behind us as I readied myself for our final trough 'dip' at Brock Troughs. Not long after passing Barton & Broughton, Harry put on the blower and shut off steam for the last time and at Oxheys Cattle Docks was braking the train hard to reduce the speed over Fylde Junction and our final stop in platform six, (Now number four) at Preston Station at 4.45am. On getting relieved by a set of shocked Edge Hill (Liverpool) men the rather young 'Scouse' fireman remarked, "Surely you don t expect me to fire this all the way to Liverpool !" to which Harry replied, "I know, it must be a strain, we've only brought it from Glasgow, one hundred and ninety eight miles away!" On arrival at home that morning I went to bed and slept for two days solid with the knowledge of knowing that only two days later, on Tuesday the 22nd of September, I would be back signing on duty at 9.45pm to work the 10.40pm. to London. Returning with the 6.30pm the following night but that's another story.

We were informed at a later date that this run from Glasgow on the 19th September 1964, with 46128 *The Lovat Scouts* was the very last time that this train was steam hauled. Such was life in the Top Link at Preston (or any other depot) and only on a weekly rate of £14.4s (£14.20p) no wonder the mileage payment came in handy but you had to sweat for it.

Plate57. 'Britannia' Class 4-6-2 Pacific No.70013, *Oliver Cromwell* (minus nameplates) is seen at Preston in February 1967 after arrival with the 00.25am Crewe-Preston parcels train. This was a running in turn for 70013, ex-works after being outshopped the previous day at Crewe Works, the last steam locomotive to be overhauled there.

Photo, J.A.Oldfield.

Plate 58. By the mid 1960's diesel locomotives had made serious inroads into the prestige steam workings over the W.C.M.L., as illustrared above with English Electric Type 4, No.D310, seen south of Warrington on the approach to Acton Grange with the Up 'Caledonian' about 1963.   Photo, Jim Carter.

Plate 59. Some workings however, continued to be worked by steam until its last days and in the mid 1960's there were still plenty of regular steam turns to be found in the North West. In March 1965, a pair of Class 5's, Nos. 45394 & 45181, are seen on Lea Green Troughs with a Manchester-Blackpool special. Photo,J.A Oldfield.

CHAPTER EIGHT
THE FINAL YEARS

Following the steam run outlined in the last chapter, on 19th September 1964, the steam locomotive fleet was being run down at an alarming rate as British Railways had their eyes on other things and my last recorded run with a steam locomotive on a passenger train was on the 10th May 1966, when I worked the 7.00am. daily stopping train to Crewe, with 'Black Five' 4-6-0 No.45118, returning to Preston with the 12.40pm. departure from Crewe hauled by 2750hp Brush/Sulzer No.D1824. My final recorded working of all, on a steam locomotive, came just over one month later, with driver Arthur Chesters and class 4, 2-6-0 No.43041 on the station pilot,. so in actual fact I finished my steam career on the same job I had started on back in January 1961.

Steam still struggled on for another twenty seven months in the North West at the last few remaining sheds including Lostock Hall, Rose Grove and Carnforth, and it must have been one of the saddest days for many footplate men on the 11th August 1968, with the very last steam run under B.R. ownership. I am sure a lot of the men felt they had lost an old and trusted friend. One day later, along with a lot of former firemen, I became known as a secondman as the title of Fireman was lost forever.

Plate 60. 9F, 2-10-0 No.92105 stands on the ashpit at at Lostock Hall whilst awaiting the attention of the 4pm. disposal crew on 19th April 1966. As can be seen in this view the environs of the ashpit were the dirtiest on a steam shed.
Photo, Mick Howarth.

Just eight months after the demise of steam, on the 4th of March 1969, I went to take my drivers examination at Preston with inspector Arthur Morris. This took almost a full day of questions and answers, but in the end he seemed satisfied with the results and I was once again promoted to the rank of 'Passed Secondman'. My first task on returning to the signing on point was to make out a route knowledge card. However, this turned out to be very sparse with only the Preston Station limits, Blackpool (North) and Huddersfield in evidence. I would still be unable to drive any sort of train until I had trained and passed out on the various types of traction units.

The first type of traction I received training on, was the Class 40, and I thought it would be impossible for the instructor to teach me anything about these locomotives, but I was proved wrong as I learned things about them I never knew existed. The training was easy compared with passing out on them with Inspector Douglas Cullen, who appeared to be rather strict on the answers to his questions. He also had an uncanny knack of getting the awkward answers from anyone. Some time later Jim Hoggarth and myself went for training on the 350hp diesel shunters and once completed we decided to have a day out at Blackpool for some dinner and a walk along the promenade. Where we came face to face with no other than Dougie Cullen and his wife. He looked rather surprised to see two of his men outside the Central Pier in full uniform, but his only comment was "I didn't know they were now running 350 shunts on the

Plate 61. The Author watches the photographer from the cab of Type 2 No25 082, ready to depart Bolton Trinity Street with the last Belfast Boat Express on 5th April 1972.   Photo, M.J.Borrowdale.

tram lines." With that we beat a rather hasty retreat back to the station.

A rather amusing incident occured one day when four of us again went to Blackpool for the day. On arrival outside the Central Pier, at the height of the holiday season, one of the lads produced a detonator from his pocket and decided to attach it to the tram line. At this moment a tram from Bispham was approaching. There was an almighty 'bang', with this, women started screaming and dogs barking. The tram driver slammed on his brakes and jumped out of his cab to investigate the cause of the commotion, but the lad was quicker and picked up the squashed detonator to replace it in his pocket. We all just stood there and watched the driver crawl under his tram to fmd out if a part had broken off or exploded.

My traction knowledge became more widespread over the following years, with the addition of classes 24, 25, 31, 37, 47 and 50 (ex D400s). Following the eventual electrification of the West Coast Main Line I also trained on the electric locos of class 81 to 90. I also learned the routes to London and Glasgow. The 6th of April 1992, was another date to remember as it was the end of the London Midland Region of British Rail. From then all workings would be taken over by private operators. I opted to transfer to Intercity Cross-Country at Preston, and soon started another training programme on the High Speed Trains (H.S.T's) to add to my already substantial traction knowledge.

Plate 62. A.C.Electric No.86 208 *City of Chester,* stands with pantograph lowered in bay 3A at Preston before its next turn of duty.
Photo, Author.

Route knowledge was also another major factor in my ambitions as up to the end I retained the route to London and Glasgow and this was soon joined by Edinburgh (Waverley), Birmingham (New St), Manchester Airport and all possible diversionary routes.

On 7th August 1996, I was taken ill and had to retire from the railway after thirty seven years on the footplate which had taken me through the great steam era and on into the times of the diesels and electrics. Changes from British Railways, London Midland Region, to British Rail and finally to Virgin Cross-Country Trains Ltd. I can always say right from being a young schoolboy who loved his trains. "Ambition Achieved."

Plate 63. The Author looks back from the cab of a Type 4, Class 47 locomotive for the right away from the guard at Preston before working an express to Blackpool North in 1983. Photo, Mick Howarth.